Ballindoon Friary, Co Sligo

ABBEYS AND FRIARIES
OF IRELAND

Mike Salter

FOLLY PUBLICATIONS

ACKNOWLEDGEMENTS

Production of this book only became possible as a result of Peter Ryder providing a large number of photographs to supplement those obtained by the author. Those of Aghaboe, Annaghdown, Baltinglass, Cashel, Castledermot, Castlelyons, Clareabbey, Clonmacnoise, Clontuskert, Dungarvan, Dunmore, Ennis, Ferns, Glenarm, Grey, Kilconnell, Kilcooly, Killone, Kilshanny, Lislaughlin, Loughrea, Molana, Monasterenenagh, Movilla, Muckross, Newtownards, Portumna, Rathkeale, Roscommon, Ross Errily, Tulsk, Waterford and Wicklow are all by Peter Ryder. Kate Miles provided pictures of Abbeydorney, Ballinskelligs, Ballyboggan, Banada, Bridgetown, Buttevant, Canon Island, Killagha, Killydonell, Meelick, and Sherkin. All other photographs were taken by the author.

The plans were all drawn by the author and are mostly based on surveys made during his many cycling trips around Ireland between 1971 and 2008. Seven plans of Cistercian abbeys and plans of the three largest Augustinian priories are shown at 1:800. The rest of the plans, including all those of friaries (except Kilcrea) are shown at 1:400. This scale is used for almost all other plans of churches in England, Wales, Scotland and Ireland in this series of books, which allows for some very useful comparisons.

Thanks are also due to those who have driven the author around on a few of the fieldtrips: Max Barfield, Penni Gillis, Jeremy Morfey, Ian Rennie, and Helen Thomas, to Paul Adkins for solving computer problems, to Paul and Allan at Aspect Design for help with the cover design and other artwork matters, and members of staff at National Monument Records at Dublin and Belfast and libraries at Belfast and Oxford.

AUTHOR'S NOTES

The aim of this book is to present information, plans and photos of as many as possible of Ireland's stock of over 200 medieval monastic houses dating from the mid 12th century, when Cistercian monks and Augustinian canons were introduced to Ireland, through to the early 16th century. Early Christian monastic sites are not included here, having already been described and illustrated in the companion volume Medieval Churches of Ireland. A few later monastic churches (mostly of Augustinian priories and including two cathedral-priories) were included in that book before it was decided to proceed with this companion volume. As a result a few buildings are included in both books but repetition has been kept to a minimum as regards both text and illustrations. See page 159 for a list of churches which one might have expected to find in this book but which are in fact included in the other volume.

ABOUT THE AUTHOR

Mike Salter is 55 and has been a professional writer and publisher since he went on the Government Enterprise Allowance Scheme for unemployed people in 1988. He is particularly interested in the planning and layout of medieval buildings and has a huge collection of plans of churches and castles he has measured during tours (mostly by bicycle and motorcycle) throughout all parts of the British Isles since 1968. Wolverhampton born and bred, Mike now lives in an old cottage beside the Malvern Hills. His other interests include walking, maps, railways, board games, morris dancing, playing percussion instruments and calling dances with an occasional folk group.

Copyright 2009 by Mike Salter   First published February 2009.
Folly Publications, Folly Cottage, 151 West Malvern Rd, Malvern, Worcs, WR14 4AY
Printed by Aspect Design, 89 Newtown Rd, Malvern, Worcs, WR14 2PD

Dominican Friary Church at Cashel, Co Tipperary

CONTENTS

Monastic Life	Page	4
Monastic Buildings	Page	10
The Suppression and Afterwards	Page	19
Gazetteer of Ulster Abbeys & Friaries	Page	20
Gazetteer of Munster Abbeys & Friaries	Page	32
Gazetteer of Leinster Abbeys & Friaries	Page	78
Gazetteer of Connacht Abbeys & Friaries	Page	114
Glossary of Terms	Page	158
Further Reading	Page	159
Index of Abbeys & Friaries	Page	160

MONASTIC LIFE

Monasticism existed in Ireland from the time of St Patrick in the 5th century and there are remains of many Early Christian monasteries which are characterised by groups of mostly small churches in association with high crosses, dry-stone huts or clochans and a round tower. Many of these sites remained in use into the late medieval period. A lot of them are described in the companion volume Medieval Churches of Ireland. This book concerns itself with the abbeys and friaries built by the various monastic orders in Ireland between the 12th and the 16th century. These buildings are very different from the early monasteries, usually having larger churches with a proper choirs and many of them have domestic buildings set around a square or oblong cloister.

By the 12th century most early monasteries in England had adopted the rule of St Benedict and built a substantial church with buildings around a cloister. This hardly happened at all in Ireland, where the early monasteries where more independent and some retained almost their original form into the medieval period, although others adopted the Augustinian rule. Benedictine communities remained rare in Ireland, and only two need mentioning here: Fore (Westmeath) and Downpatrick (Down).

The rule created by St Benedict in the 6th century allowed for a daily routine with up to seven services, with some variance according to the season of the year and certain feast days requiring special services, extra masses or processions. Certain monks of each community must have been excused from some services in order to carry out specific duties and offices, although most of the menial tasks, including cooking, were to be carried out by servants. The day started with Matins at midnight which was quickly followed by Lauds, then the monks were allowed the second part of their sleep for four or five hours before returning to church for Prime. Reading time, plus the all-important masses for the souls of benefactors and their families, and some light refreshment followed, then the Lady Mass. Afterwards the monks gathered in the chapter house to firstly hear read a portion of the rule under which they lived. Weekly duties were then allocated, faults were corrected and any business conducted relating to such matters as administration of estates, construction or repair of buildings, appointment of officers or the admission of novices. The next service, Tierce or High Mass might be followed by a procession around the church and cloister. The monks then took their main meal of the day in the refectory. A good choice of foodstuffs was on offer, although it did not include meat, which was only served to sick and elderly monks in the infirmary. Monks were not allowed to indulge in idle chat during meals and were obliged to listen to one of their number reading religious tracts from a pulpit in the refectory. Afternoons were used for study, writing, the teaching of novices, short periods of recreation or just a nap during the longer days of the summer. A second meal was taken after Vespers or Evensong and after Compline the monks would retire to bed for three hours or so for the first part of their sleep until wakened for Matins.

Killagha Priory, Co Kerry

MONASTIC LIFE 5

Inch Abbey, Co Down *The nave at Kilcooly Abbey, Co Tipperary*

An order of monks to have great significance in Ireland were the Cistercians. This order began in France at the beginning of the 12th century and expended rapidly under St Bernard. They so impressed St Malachy, Archbishop of Armagh that he founded an abbey for them at Mellifont in 1142. It grew rapidly and within a few years had sent out colonies to found five daughter houses, and one of these, Monasteranenagh (Limerick) itself had two daughter houses by the mid 1150s. Many new Cistercian houses were founded in the period 1180-1200 and by 1230 there were about forty houses, although some ranked only as cells and one or two proved to be rather short-lived.

The Cistercians wore white (ie undyed) habits and were more strict, although their daily life largely followed the sort of pattern just described. Their buildings and furnishings were supposed to be kept plain and simple. They preferred remote locations away from towns and liked to be self-sufficient, becoming noted for their agricultural methods and large flocks of sheep. They recruited large numbers of lay brothers to do the manual work and established houses in the most difficult places where great works of clearance or drainage might be required. The lay brothers took the same vows of poverty, chastity and obedience and had their own parts of the monastery away from the choir-monks, and, of course, they attended less services. The Cistercians were unable to keep to their original ideals. Some of their houses soon proved so successful in their agricultural activities that they became wealthy. In later years paid servants were needed to do the manual work as it became difficult to recruit lay brothers after wars and pestilence in the first half of the 14th century reduced the population and labourers generally were in short supply and could expect better pay and conditions.

Other orders of monks such as the Cluniacs (reformed Benedictines), the Tironesians, and the hermit-like Carthusians made little impact in Ireland. A few very ruined churches remain from preceptories of the Knights Templars and the Knights Hospitallers connected with the crusades of the 12th and 13th centuries aimed at securing access for Christians to the Holy City of Jerusalem, but none of these sites have any surviving domestic buildings, although defensive walls and towers remain at Mourne.

6 MONASTIC LIFE

Clareabbey, Co Clare

A very popular order in Ireland were the Augustinian regular canons, known as the Black Canons from the colour of their habits. Reformers of the 11th century had moulded the writings of St Augustine of Hippo into a rule which could be followed by religious houses. Canons were priests, whereas the majority of monks were not, and canons mixed more with the common folk since they went out to conduct services in the many parish churches under their control and they also ran hospitals, schools and guest houses. Regular canons lived in monasteries in the same way as monks and again took the basic vows of poverty, chastity and obedience. Some of the Early Christian monasteries adopted the Augustinian rule in the 12th century and Augustinian regular canons also served the cathedrals of Christ Church in Dublin and Newtown Trim. Other cathedrals were served by secular canons, who did not lead a monastic life. The numerous (supposedly over 200) Augustinian houses in Ireland were generally small and poorly endowed. Most of them ranked only as priories with a prior as the head, although the Irish have traditionally always referred to these establishments (and those of friars) as abbeys. Only about a dozen Augustinian houses in Ireland retain evidence of a full monastic layout with ranges round a cloister, Annaghdown (Galway) Athassel (Tipperary), Ballintubber (Mayo), Bridgetown (Cork), Canon Island (Clare), Cong (Mayo), Devenish (Fermanagh) and Kells (Kilkenny) being prime examples.

Little remains of the seven houses in Ireland of the rather more austere Premonstratension regular canons who wore white habits since they modelled their constitution on that of the Cistercian monks. Their Irish houses were small and poor, lay in remote locations and none of them retain a full regular layout of buildings around a cloister. Adare has the only Irish house of Trinitarian canons.

Abbey Derg, Co Longford

Cloister arcade at Adare Franciscan Friary

In the 13th century the various orders of friars appeared in Ireland. The Dominicans arrived in the 1220s and eventually had over forty houses. The Franciscans or Grey Friars (from the colour of their habits) arrived in 1232 and had over a hundred houses, although only about half of them ever had a full layout of buildings around a cloister and this total includes thirty houses of the Third Order Franciscans. These orders were missionary preachers whose purpose was to minister to the poverty stricken masses both spiritually and physically. Consequently their houses were initially in towns, particularly the towns under Anglo-Norman control, although they were established in Ennis (Clare), a Gaelic speaking area, as early as the 1240s. Quite a number of towns, such as Adare (Limerick) and Kilkenny had more than one friary (sometimes in addition to a Cistercian abbey or a priory of one of the orders of regular canons as well) as a result of differing benefactors favouring one order over another. The Carmelite or White Friars, which eventually had two dozen Irish houses arrived c1260, and there were twenty houses of the Eremite (Augustinian) Friars who also arrived about that time. These were more contemplative orders. Just one (at Newtown Trim) now survives of twelve Irish houses of the Cross-Bearers or Crutched Friars.

The friars professed absolute poverty and relied on alms and oblations, a system which usually worked well because they remained popular with both the masses and the upper classes. Monks and both regular and secular canons were less keen on friars, especially the Franciscans, who were accused of giving absolution too easily. Friars were keen on learning and teaching and did not always own friaries, which were sometimes built and maintained by benefactors. Friaries were not usually endowed with lands or appropriated parish churches for financial support. The majority of friars were based in convents and had a life not unlike that of monks and regular canons but a few friars had licence to travel and preach without being attached to a monastery.

MONASTIC LIFE

Grey Abbey, Co Down from the SE, showing the refectory south gable

Only a few new Irish monasteries were founded during the 14th century. However, quite a number of new houses for friars were founded in the Gaelic-speaking areas of western Ireland during the second half of the 15th century. Towns were few and far between in these areas and the new friaries lie in open countryside. Some of the new houses were for Franciscan Observants who went back to the original basic and strict rules of the order. Others were for Third Order Franciscans (the Second Order being nuns) in which married people could lead a life according to Franciscan principles.

Priory at Devenish, Co Fermanagh

Most orders of monks, regular canons and friars also had houses of nuns. Females did not go out preaching but Franciscan and Dominican nuns administered to the sick. Nunneries held few attractions for potential male benefactors and were never numerous in medieval Ireland. No Irish nunnery ever attained anything like the size and importance that a few of the Benedictine and Augustinian nunneries did in England. Several of the Early Christian monastic settlements had an outlying church (usually dedicated to St Mary) for the use of either women in general or nuns specifically (it is usually difficult to know which). The Augustinians had twenty nunneries in Ireland but remains of them are minimal and Killone and Monasternagalliaghduff are the only ones with surviving domestic ranges. The latter has a very unusual layout with a simple oblong church projecting from the eastern side of the cloister.

A large monastery could have quite a number of officials under the abbot as head, and the prior and sub-prior as second and third in command, although Irish houses tended to be smaller than their European counterparts, perhaps needing less officials. Church services were organised and managed by the precentor, who was the chief singer and also the librarian and archivist. He had an assistant called the succentor. The sacrist looked after the fabric of the church and its ornaments, vestments and furnishings, usually having an office beside or near the east end of the church. His deputy the sub-sacrist rang the bells to summon the brethren to services. The cellarer was in charge of supplies of food and drink, often extending to dominion over the mills, brew-house and agricultural work at the abbey's possessions, although these might be looked after by a lay steward, whilst the sub-cellarer or kitchener had responsibility for the preparation and cooking of food. The fraterer was in charge of serving the food and drink and the cleaning of the refectory and the lavatory outside it where the monks washed their hands before eating (Mellifont has a fine lavatory). A chamberlain was in charge of providing bedding, hot water for shaving and occasional baths, and the provision of clothing for the brethren. Novice monks usually used some of the lower rooms in the east range and were under the supervision of novice-master. Sick and elderly monks went to an infirmary separate from the main buildings (usually further east). It was looked after by another official and was the only place where meat other than fish was served. If the house was wealthy enough to have a guest house another official was required to administer it. Posts such as an almoner in charge of distributing money and surplus food to the poor, and a school-master may have been rarer in Ireland on account of the Augustinian houses being small and poor and the Cistercian abbeys being mostly located far from centres of population that might benefit from such services. Although idle conversation was discouraged by monastic rules all these officials would have needed to liaise with each other and various other monks every day and to give instructions to a large number of paid laymen servants.

The screen at Clontuskert Abbey, Co Galway

MONASTIC BUILDINGS

The standard layout which had evolved for Continental monasteries during the 9th and 10th centuries was in general use in England by the late 11th century and reached Ireland in the mid 12th century with the Cistercians. Their churches followed a very standardised plan and were usually cruciform with barrel-vaulted subsidiary chapels approximately square in plan opening off the eastern sides of the cross-arms or transepts. The chapels contained some of the many extra altars that were needed so that all the monks who were priests could perform mass in person at an altar. The high altar lay at the east end of a short presbytery which was often vaulted and lower roofed than the nave and transepts. In Cistercian houses the monks' choir lay in the eastern bays of the nave to the west of the central crossing, but in churches of other orders with longer eastern arms and shorter naves the choir often lay at least partly under the central crossing arches. The Cistercian General Chapter banned towers in 1157 but this rule tended to be ignored and by the early 13th century several of their English and Irish abbeys had a low and plain pyramidal-roofed central tower set over the four crossing arches, as at Boyle. The rest of the nave contained the choir stalls and altar of the lay-brothers. Cistercian naves usually had side aisles with arcades of between six and eight bays and were lighted by a triplet of lancet windows in the west wall and a series of lancets above the piers of the arcades to form a clerestory. Grey Abbey is an unusual case of a Cistercian nave without aisles, but aisle-less naves were common in Augustinian churches, where they were often used by laymen. One bay of the nave between the monks' choir and the lay brothers' choir was usually screened off with two walls supporting a loft, the west of which had a rood or crucifix, whilst the other side had lecterns for the reading of the Gospel and Epistle, hence the name pulpitum usually given to this structure. The stalls occupied by the abbot and prior backed onto the pulpitum, set either side of a passage beneath it and facing the high altar, but most of the other stalls backed onto screens under the arcades and thus faced each other.

Church at Hospital, Co Limerick

Hore Abbey and the Rock of Cashel, Co Tipperary

Monasteranenagh Abbey, Co Limerick

Two of the early Cistercian houses had rare deviations from standard planning with regard to the transept eastern chapels. At Mellifont four of the six chapels were apsed (they were a rarity in Ireland and were replaced by square chapels in a later rebuilding) and at Baltinglass each chapel projected separately, a layout also found in the mid 13th century in the cathedral of Cashel. Commonly there were four chapels (two to each transept) but Duiske, Dunbrody and Monasternenagh had six and the small church at Corcomroe only two. Not all monastic churches were cruciform. The Augustinians often built churches with just a nave and chancel, or a simple plain oblong. The latter was also the form of the modest 13th century churches at the Benedictine priory of Fore and the Augustinian nunnery of Monasternagalliaghduff. At Inishmaine and Dungiven chancels were added to older naves in the early 13th century, and O'Heyne's church at Kilmacduagh has a nave and chancel which are both early 13th century.

In Augustinian, Benedictine and Cistercian abbeys the cloister was usually located on the sunny south side of the nave and had four lean-to roofed walks with open arcades. These arcades very seldom remained intact after the buildings were abandoned. What remains is mostly 15th century, as at Bective, Holy Cross and Jerpoint. The northern walk was often a study area with a library kept close at hand in cupboards in the south transept west wall. The other cloister walks formed communicating passages. There was always a doorway into the church from the cloister NE corner, and often one at the NW corner as well. The range on the east side of the cloister had the monks' dormitory on the upper storey with a direct stair into the south transept for use at night, whilst a staircase further south was used during the daytime. The dormitory was originally one single huge room but later on it was commonly subdivided by wooden screens into cubicles. At the south end of the dormitory would be the reredorter or latrine set over a carefully made drainage channel. Occasionally to facilitate such drainage the plan would be reversed with the cloister set on the north side of the church, as at Hore. Below the dormitory were several rooms which were often covered with vaulting. The sacristy for storing the church plate and vestments would be next to the transept, then the chapter house where the monks met to hear read a chapter of the rule of their order and then discuss the business of the abbey. Chapter houses sometimes extended further east than the rest of the east range and often had a sumptuous entrance portal flanked by a smaller opening on each side. Next would usually be a passageway leading out to the cemetery further east. The rest of the range contained one or two rooms which seem to have been used for the instruction of novices.

12 MONASTIC BUILDINGS

Corcomroe Abbey, Co Clare

Monastic refectories usually spacious, well-lighted and fitted with a stone pulpit for a reader. They were usually located on the opposite side of the cloister from the church, where there was sometimes a lavatory for the washing of hands, a fine example remaining at Mellifont. The Cistercians differed from other orders in that they preferred the refectory to extend at right angles to the cloister, i.e. parallel to the dormitory although this practice only seems to have been adhered to in less than half of their Irish abbeys. This layout allowed space for a kitchen on the west side of it and a calefactory or warming house on the east. In Cistercian houses the western range contained the lay-brothers' dormitory set over their refectory and stores and perhaps an office for the cellarer. In houses of other orders this range often contained rooms for the head of the house (originally they were supposed to sleep in the dormitory with the other monks), and rooms for guests set over offices and stores. The infirmary would be a separate group of buildings including a hall, chapel and kitchen usually located to the east or SE of the main dormitory and by the later medieval period the abbot might also have his own house in this area. Outbuildings such as workshops and barns were sometimes timber-framed and have left few traces. The bakehouse to the SW of the cloister at Inch (Down) is a rare exception. However the gatehouse of the precinct wall survives in a few instances, notably Athassel.

Even if a monastery was well endowed and could afford to employ a large team of workmen and craftsmen it usually took up to fifty years or more to gradually replace an initial series of temporary huts with a full layout of church and claustral buildings built of mortared stone. Work on the church usually progressed from east to west so that the altar and choir spaces were roofed first, then the east range would be built, then the refectory and cloister, and then the west range. In small and poorly endowed monasteries funds soon ran low and the west range was either never added, or only after a gap of several decades or even centuries. By the time a west range had been added the oldest parts often needed rebuilding or enlarging or it was simply decided to remodel them in the latest architectural style.

MONASTIC BUILDINGS   13

Double piscina at Kilconnell   *Long row of lancets at Bridgetown, Co Cork*

Although work had begun on several Cistercian abbeys in Ireland by the 1150s there is now little standing walling at any of them which predates the period 1180-1210. This period, which also coincides with the Anglo-Norman conquest of the eastern two thirds of Ireland, and the foundation of many new Cistercian and Augustinian houses, produced architecture which is transitional in style between the round arched Romanesque and the first phase of Gothic using the pointed arch. At Baltinglass there are round arches into the transepts and a pointed-arched arcade with Romanesque type scalloped capitals on the alternately round and square piers. Boyle has a round-arched south arcade and a pointed-arched north arcade of about the same period and the west window is a pointed-headed lancet adorned with chevrons, a Romanesque motif. The nave at Jerpoint has Romanesque capitals on piers supporting a pointed-arched arcade. Here the eastern parts of the church may actually go back to the 1160s. The east wall at Knockmoy of c1210 has an old fashioned arrangement of a row of three quite modest round-headed windows of equal height and a slightly larger single lancet above, whilst another lancet lighted an attic room over the presbytery vault. The nave arcades have pointed arches set on long rectangular piers. The church of the Augustinian house at Ballintober has a similar layout with triple round-arched east windows with some chevrons but the nave has no aisles. The windows are roll-moulded in a manner often found in the western parts of Ireland, as in the smaller Augustinian nave and chancel churches at Inishmaine and Kilmacduagh.

Canon Island Priory, Co Clare   *Abbeydorney, Co Kerry*

14 MONASTIC BUILDINGS

The Cistercian abbeys of Corcomroe, Duiske, Dunbrody, Grey and Inch have churches of the first years of the 13th century. Each has a triplet of tall lancet windows in the east wall of the church, the middle one taller than the other two at Duiske, Dunbrody and Inch, and at Grey there is a similar triplet in the south gable of the refectory. At Duiske the rere-arches of the windows are trefoiled, an advanced design, whilst the processional doorway towards the cloister is still round-headed, as are the two outer lancets of the triplet. Of the same period are fine remains of the Augustinian house at Cong, where more survives of the walls around the cloister with a spectacular chapter house entrance and a reset processional doorway. Athassel of perhaps the 1230s has the largest of the Augustinian churches (except for cathedral-priories) and the most complete set of claustral buildings, outbuildings and precinct walls of houses of this order. Both here and at Kells (which also has fine later medieval precinct walls with residential towers) a bell-tower is located at the NW corner of the church. The nave is of later in the 13th century, as is the Cistercian church at Tintern formerly with Geometrical tracery in the east window, buttresses surmounted by gablets and a central tower later heightened with multi-stepped battlements.

The Augustinian priory of St John at Kilkenny has a pair of late 13th century windows composed of stepped triple groups of trefoil-headed lancets. Other windows of that period took the form of two lancets placed together with a circle or quatrefoil between their heads (Irish examples are rare) and from this developed the tracery forms of the 14th and 15th centuries. Intersecting or switchline tracery was introduced c1300 and in Ireland remained in fashion throughout the late medieval period, as did occasional large windows of several lights with reticulation or floral tracery patterns. Windows of two ogival-headed lights set under a hoodmould were common in the 15th century, both in churches and in domestic buildings. Jerpoint broke the Cistercian convention of austere and simple architectural forms in the early 14th century by inserting a new east window adorned with ball-flowers and three cusped lights below a circle once filled with whirling, cusped comma-shaped lights. It then compounded this in the 15th century by raising an embattled tower with corner turrets over the crossing.,

Choir at Athassel Priory, Co Tipperary   *Doorway at Athassel Priory*

Doorway at Cong Abbey   *Sedile & piscina at Monasternagalliaghduff*

Some abbeys such as Kilcooly and Holy Cross saw major rebuilding in the 15th century. Both (but especially Holy Cross) have many fine late medieval windows using tracery forms such as intersection with or without mouchettes (foiled dagger-shapes) and reticulation. The Perpendicular style used in England from the late 14th to the early 16th century is hardly ever seen in late medieval Irish abbeys and friaries. However many of the Cistercian houses were in a state of decline by the 15th century with only a handful of monks and only minimal agricultural activity. The expense of maintaining large churches proved prohibitive in an era when benefactors tended to favour friars who served the general population rather than monks who shut themselves away for contemplation in a retreat. At Bective, Corcomroe and Jerpoint the naves each lost an aisle during a remodelling amounting to down-sizing and at several houses such as Monasternenagh and Inch the transepts and most of the nave and its aisles were walled off and left to decay. Something similar happened to the cathedral-priories at Downpatrick and Newtown Trim. A number of monasteries under English control but outside of the English Pale became fortresses in the late medieval period, notably Fore. Kells and Athassel already had defensible precincts, whilst combined residential and defensive towers were added at others such as the hospital at Newtown Trim and the priory of Ballybeg. Common late medieval alterations in the claustral buildings of older abbeys included inserting crosswalls and adding a small latrine projections.

Western view of the Franciscan Friary at Askeaton, Co Limerick

16 MONASTIC BUILDINGS

Cloister arcades at the Augustinian Friary at Adare, Co Limerick

Friaries have a rather different layout from the Cistercian and Augustinian houses. The cloister is usually small and almost always set on the north side (exceptions were the Franciscan houses at Askeaton, Castledermot and Nenagh and the Dominican house at Athenry). The refectory is thus usually in the north range and is sometimes on an upper storey extending over vaulted store-rooms and the northern alley of the cloister, whilst the dormitory likewise may extend over the eastern alley of the cloister, and other narrow vaulted rooms in the east range. Where this is the case the cloister alleys are vaulted and the arcades are strengthened with buttressing to carry the upper storey walls. There is not always a room which is identifiable as a chapter house. Most of the claustral buildings which survive at Irish friaries are 15th century, even in older friaries with 13th or 14th century work remaining in their churches.

Initially friary churches were simple long oblongs with the east wall filled with a stepped series of three or five lancets with triangular piers between them so that they are conjoined internally but appear separate from the outside. At the Franciscan church at Nenagh the lancets are enormous and there is hardly any solid wall below the gable. A feature particularly characteristic of 13th century friary churches is a long regularly spaced row of lancet windows with just shafts between their embrasures internally. There is a row of eleven on the north side at Nenagh. There are nine on the south side at Cashel, eight on the south side at Sligo, and seven on the north side at Athenry. These three, along with the more altered church at Roscommon, are all Dominican friary churches of the 1240s and 50s. There are also a row of nine lancets at the Franciscan friary at Ardfert. Other early Franciscan churches of note include those of Buttevant (with a row of round-headed lancets), Castledermot, Claregalway, Ennis, Kilkenny and Waterford. Kilkenny has a group of seven stepped east lancets divided only by mullions, probably of c1300, whilst Ennis has a group of five of about the same period with only the central three grouped together with just slender mullions between them. Dominican churches of c1270 at Lorrha and Rathfran have regularly spaced double lancets along one side, whilst that at Kilmallock of c1300 has a regular row of two-light windows with Y-tracery along one side and there is an east window of five graduated lancets divided only by mullions.

Two Augustinian friary churches have good early 14th century windows. There are ones with intersecting tracery at Adare, and two at Fethard with cusped Geometrical tracery and cusped intersecting tracery. The Franciscan church at Castledermot was given a large north transept with side chapels and a large end window with complex tracery, and another large window was provided in an extension to the choir. An extension of the 1320s to the Dominican church at Athenry has a multifoiled circle above trefoiled lights in a south window and a sex-foiled spherical triangle in the north window. The destroyed east window was of five lights with intersecting tracery and other motifs. The nave was given a four light window with intersecting and many pointed trefoils and also gained a north aisle and a transept with a west aisle. A large transept added to the Dominican church at Kilkenny probably in the 1340s has a five-light end window with complex Decorated style tracery and a row of side-windows of three lights with a variety of tracery forms. Other early 14th century additions include an aisle with round piers at Claregalway and a transept with a west aisle at Kilmallock. The only work of significance thought to be late 14th century is the Augustinian friary church at Clonmines, which has a short south aisle and the remains of a very large east window.

The founders and principal benefactors of monasteries usually expected two principal personal services in return in addition to the general benefits such as caring for the sick that monastic communities often provided to the common folk of the locality. Firstly they asked for masses to be celebrated to help their souls in the afterlife, and secondly they used monastic churches as burial places, especially in Ireland where there are very few major monuments within the ordinary parish churches, most of which are small and fairly plain. Tomb recesses are very common in monastic churches and some of them are extremely ornate, but few of the effigies and tombs they contained have survived. Effigies or tombs either complete or fragmentary remain at Corcomroe, Ennis, Jerpoint, Kilcooly, Kilconnell, Kilmallock, Strade and in the cathedral priory at Dublin. Stained glass windows also could provide memorials, but none of these have survived as they were too easily damaged. Occasionally architectural features such the west doorway at Clontuskert are provided with inscriptions and coats of arms,

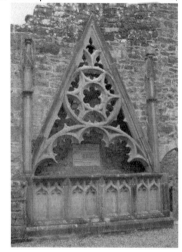

Detail of a monument at Strade Friary, Co Mayo   *Tomb at Kilconnell Friary, Co Galway*

MONASTIC BUILDINGS

Friary churches often had a thin tower set upon two cross-walls pierced by arches taking the place of the original rood screen and pulpitum between the friars' choir and the nave used by laymen. Even in friaries newly founded in the 15th century such a tower was usually a later insertion. In Franciscan churches the upper stages of the tower were commonly reduced to a square, often of great height, above a rectangular base across the internal width of the church. The towers of the Dominican church at Drogheda and the Franciscan church at Kilkenny are thought to be of c1340 but the other towers appear to be 15th century. The Kilkenny tower appears to be one of the earliest examples, either secular or ecclesiastical, with the type of stepped battlements characteristic of Irish late medieval buildings. Spaces under towers usually have rib-vaults and east and west arches with a chamfered inner order carried on brackets.

Often a sacristy which could be of two storeys was set beside the eastern end of the north wall of the choir. Otherwise the southernmost room of the east range lowest storey was used as a sacristy. Occasionally an aisle was later added on the side of the nave away from the cloister, but a more usual addition in friaries was a very large transept long enough to contain two or three altars along its east wall. Sometimes this wall is thickened to contain two altar recesses with a tiny storeroom between them as at Rathfran and Moyne (both in Mayo). In a few instances there are proper projecting chapels instead of recesses, as in the Franciscan friary at Adare (Limerick), where the chapels have tomb recesses and the northern one is longer than the other, and there is a west aisle to the transept as well as a south aisle to the nave.

Most of the friary churches (and the abbey churches as well) have piscinae for rinsing vessels after mass both at the east end of the south wall and in the east walls of transepts. In the south wall there are often two or three sedilia or seats for officiating priests. Those in friaries are usually fairly modest (see below) but the abbey at Holy Cross has a particularly ornate set. Friary churches of the late 15th century often have windows with intersecting tracery with round sub-arches over the main lights.

Sedilia in the choir at the Franciscan Friary at Adare, Co Limerick

THE SUPPRESSION AND AFTERWARDS

In 1536 an Irish Parliament proclaimed Henry VIII of England as supreme head of the Church of Ireland. Eight decayed monasteries were immediately dissolved and an Act of Suppression dissolved another fourteen in 1537. The rest were officially dissolved under a further act in 1539. A commission set up in 1540 to survey dissolved abbey estates and estimate the value of the rents and revenues was empowered to lease former abbeys to trustworthy (i.e. Protestant) laymen. By 1541 most monasteries in the east parts of Ireland and in towns, where the Crown's authority was most effective, had been dissolved. New owners of former Cistercian abbeys at Bective, Dunbrody and Tintern converted parts of them into residences. In other places, especially in towns, all re-usable materials such as lead, timber and stone were sold and removed.

In the western Gaelic-speaking parts of Ireland the Crown's authority was minimal and the suppression of monasteries proved more difficult. Even after the Gaelic chiefs were induced to surrender their lands and receive them back with new titles they remained very independent. Even those that nominally adopted Protestantism were reluctant to move friars off their lands. In the conflicts of the 1570s and 80s friars were chased out of their buildings by English forces, and some even put to death, but the survivors always returned when it was safe to do so. Only rarely in these areas were friary buildings deliberately dismantled. Occasionally a friary would be set on fire, thus destroying the roofs, but afterwards it was still possible for friars to live amongst any vaulted lower rooms and occasionally even re-roof a small part. Only one friary, Rathmullen in Donegal, was eventually converted into a private residence.

Banishment of all Catholic priests and friars proclaimed in 1605 and new plantations after the earls of Tyrone and Tyrconnell fled to Spain in 1607 failed to stop the friars. In 1613 it was reported that Catholics in Ireland had "re-edified monasteries wherin friars publicly preach and say mass". In Co Galway six friars were still active at Ross Errily in 1615, and about that time the Dowager Countess of Clanrickarde had at least part of the friary at Kilnalahan re-roofed. At that time there were still a few Cistercian monks at Corcomroe, and Augustinian regular canons appear to recovered Ballintubber in the 1630s. Even after being chased out by Cromwellian soldiers in the wars of 1648-52 friars remained in the vicinity of their houses, and in some cases re-occupied parts of them. There had been a Catholic resurgence in 1642-5, when forces of the Confederate Catholics took possession of cathedrals at Limerick and Kilkenny, and part of the ruined cathedral at Kilmacduagh was re-roofed by a Catholic bishop in 1647-9, whilst in 1644 the newly repaired Dominican friary at Athenry became a Catholic university. A few friars still remained at Claregalway, Moyne and Ross Errilly as late as the 1750s.

The churches and domestic buildings at ten Franciscan friaries at Adare, Askeaton, Creevelea, Kilcrea, Moyne, Muckross, Quin, Rosserk, Ross Errily and Timoleague all in the west and SW of Ireland have survived in a remarkably complete state, mostly lacking only their roofs. All these and indeed almost all Irish monastic remains are national monuments, most of them lying in graveyards which have remained in use with free unrestricted public access. Ruins at Boyle, Jerpoint, Sligo and Tintern are monuments where admission fees are charged. Very little of importance is not publicly accessible.

Since 1800 a number of monastic churches have been restored as Catholic parish churches, as at Adare, Ballintober, Fethard and Kilkenny. In 1827 Franciscan friars restored the friary at Multyfarnham from which they had only been finally ejected by the Cromwellians in 1651, whilst the Cistercian abbey church at Holy Cross was re-roofed in the 1970s. A third former monastic church at Adare is now used by Protestants and a school was set up in the restored domestic buildings. A Franciscan friary in Waterford was for a while used for worship by French Protestant refugees.

ULSTER ABBEYS AND FRIARIES

ARMAGH FRIARY   Co Armagh   H876447   To SE of the cathedral and town

Within the grounds of the archbishop's palace are remains of the 49m long church of a Franciscan friary founded in 1264 by Archbishop O'Scannail and later patronised by the O'Donnells. Parts of the west end remain, with two arches of an arcade towards a former south aisle, and there are low fragments further east. The domestic buildings were destroyed by Sean O'Neill in 1561 to prevent them holding an English garrison.

ASSAROE ABBEY   Co Donegal   G870623   1km NW of Ballyshannon

Just two lengths of walling 9m high remain of a Cistercian abbey founded in 1178 by Flaharty O'Muldorry as a daughter house of Boyle in Roscommon. It was ransacked in 1398 and occupied by the English in 1597, but the community survived until 1607.

BALLEEGHAM FRIARY   Co Donegal   C253150   3km NNE of Manorcunningham

An ivy-covered church 25m by 6m internally remains of a Franciscan Third Order friary founded by the O'Donnells in the late 15th century. In 1603 it was suppressed and the lands given to James Fullerton. The three-light east window with Flamboyant tracery is the best of its type in Ulster. A two light south window also remains near the east end, and there are other windows further west. An unusual feature is the doorway on the south side of the nave in addition to the usual west doorway which faces the sea.

BALLYSAGGART FRIARY
Co Donegal   G746718

5km SW of Dunkineely

The MacSwiney Banaghs are thought to have founded this Franciscan Third Order friary c1500. The community was disbanded after the O'Neills and O'Donnells were defeated at Kinsale in 1602. An oblong church 20m long by 6m wide internally remains with a good two-light east window. There were sedilia below the SE window.

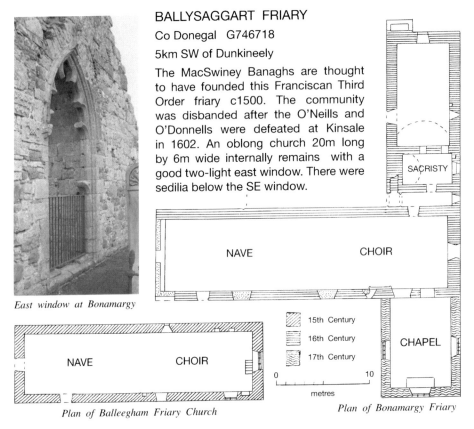

East window at Bonamargy

Plan of Balleegham Friary Church

Plan of Bonamargy Friary

ULSTER ABBEYS & FRIARIES 21

Bangor Abbey

Armagh Friary

BANGOR ABBEY   Co Down   J501811   To SW of town centre

Bangor had an important monastery founded by St Comgall c555-9 but it decayed later on, partly a result of Viking raids. In 1137 Mael M'Aedhog resigned as archbishop of Armagh and re-established the abbey of Bangor (of which he had become abbot in 1124) as a house of Arroasion Augustinian regular canons. He died here in 1148, having established a new see which was transferred to Downpatrick by the Norman invader John de Courcy in 1177. The abbey was transferred to Franciscan control in 1469 because it was decayed, and it was suppressed in 1542. Little remains of it apart from the tower between the nave and the chancel of the church. Now equipped with a balustrade and spire, it forms a west tower to the present Church of Ireland church.

BONAMARGY FRIARY   Co Antrim   D126409   0.5km E of of Ballycastle

Rory MacQuillan is thought to have founded this Franciscan Third Order friary c1500. It was burned in 1584 when an Irish and Scottish force attacked English troops quarters in the friary, but it was repaired and remained in use by Franciscans doing missionary work in western Scotland after the friars of the Third Order withdrew in the early 17th century. The church is 30m long by 7.5m wide internally and has a doorway and three large blocked windows plus one open smaller one on the south side and an east window which once had three lights with arched lights below a transom and Flamboyant tracery at the top. The north wall was left blank for a cloister although it appears that the surviving east range was all that was ever built, at least in stone. Set over a passage, a sacristy and a large room, all vaulted, is a dormitory probably once divided into cubicles for six friars, with a latrine at the north end. To the east is a fragmentary gatehouse which had an upper room in the roof. To the south of the east end of the church is a 17th century chapel with three windows of four lights set over the burial vault of the MacDonnells, the presence of which probably accounts for the building having remained in use as late as the end of the 17th century. It is dated 1621 but may actually be rather later. Nearby on the south wall is the MacNaghten tomb of 1630.

CORICKMORE FRIARY   Co Tyrone   H452881   5.5km ENE of Newtownstewart

Overgrown ruins of an oblong church of a Franciscan Third Order friary stand on a promontory above the confluence of the Owenkillew and Glenelly Rivers. The friary was founded c1465 and remained in use until 1603, when it was granted to Sir Henry Piers. A description of 1837 suggests that domestic buildings then still remained.

22 ULSTER ABBEYS & FRIARIES

DEVENISH PRIORY Co Fermanagh   H224469   On an island in Lough Erne

Two separate monasteries stood side by side on this island and both survived until the early 17th century. One had a church, an oratory and a round tower and was held by a sect of the Culdees who had taken over a monastery originally founded in the 6th century by St Molaise. The other was an Augustinian priory of St Mary founded in 1130. It was supposedly provided with a new church in 1449, when Bartholomew O'Flannagan was prior, but there was much rebuilding about fifty years later following a fire. The church measures 28m by 7m internally but the walls are now much reduced except for the choir north wall with a pinnacled and foliated doorway to a sacristy and the vaulted central tower set on two arches with ashlar piers. The inner orders of these arches spring from brackets. The east window has been taken off to the church at Monea. To the north was a cloister with a chapter house in the east range, a refectory in the north range, and a guest house in the west range, now mostly reduced to footings. See p8.

DONEGAL FRIARY Co Donegal   G927780   0.5km SW of Donegal

Hugh O'Donnell and his wife Nuala O'Brien founded this Franciscan Friary in 1474 and it is assumed to have had a complete set of buildings by 1488 when it was the venue for an important provincial chapter of the order. Friars remained here until 1601 when most of the buildings were destroyed in an explosion whilst Niall Garbh O'Donnell was holding the friary against an attack by his cousin Hugh. In 1607 the friary was granted to Sir Basil Brooke, who created a new house within the nearby castle of the O'Donnells, but the community still remained in the vicinity in the 1630s when four of its members wrote their Annals which survive to give us much historical information.

Of a church 45m long internally there remain most of the choir, although without much detail, the end wall of the south transept, which had a large eastern chapel, and part of the north wall of the nave. There was a central tower and a south aisle with a four bay arcade, the easternmost arch opening into the transept. Parts of the north and east arcades remain of a small cloister on the north. The east arcade has pointed arches on paired octagonal shafts and had a buttress in the middle. The round-arched north arcade is inferior work, probably of 16th century date. The south alley had a lean-to roof but the others had rooms above, with a dormitory on the east and a refectory on the north. Part remains of the latrine block at the NE corner, and there was a kitchen at the NW corner, and a sacristy east of the south end of the east range. A wide stair lay near the kitchen and the narrow dormitory stair remains within the choir north wall

Donegal Friary

ULSTER ABBEYS & FRIARIES 23

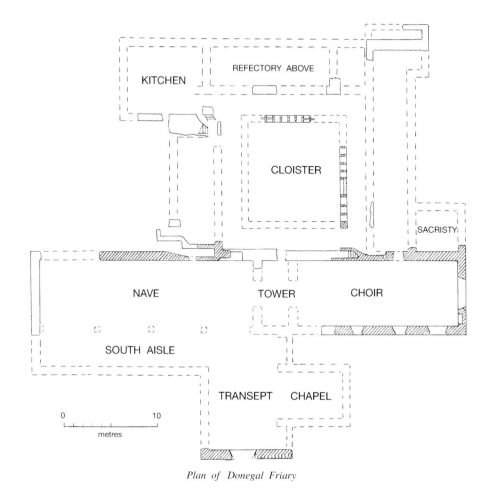

Plan of Donegal Friary

DUNGIVEN PRIORY   Co Londonderry   C692083   To S of town of Dungiven

In the 1150s Augustinian canons took over an existing church with one 12th century window still surviving. The chancel added in the 13th century has two east lancets and a tomb of one of the 15th century O'Cahan patrons on the south side. It was once vaulted. The church became parochial in 1603 and the west tower then became part of a house and bawn built by Sir Edward Doddington, whose widow remained in residence until the Irish captured the placed in 1641. For a plan and photos see the companion volume Medieval Churches of Ireland.

GLENARM FRIARY   Co Antrim   D310154   At Glenarn, 3km SE of Carnlough

By the Protestant church are meagre footings of a Franciscan Third Order friary founded in 1465 by Robert Bisset. In it Sean the Proud O'Neill was buried in 1567.

West doorway at Grey Abbey

Grey Abbey

GREY ABBEY Co Down   J583682   To east of village, NE of Strangford Lough

This Cistercian abbey was founded in 1193 by Affreca, wife of John de Courcy and daughter of the King of Man in gratitude for having survived a stormy sea journey. The monks came from Holm Cultram in Cumbria. In the later medieval period the O'Neills of Clandeboye were patrons but when dissolved in 1541 the abbey was poor and decayed. The buildings seem to have survived until burned in the conflicts of the 1570s. After being granted to Sir Hugh Montgomery in 1607 the church was re-roofed and used for parish worship until 1778. The ruins were taken into state care in 1907.

The chief features of the church are the two rows of triple lancet windows at the east end, where there is also a piscina and sedile, and the unusually fine west doorway with four moulded orders (one with dogtooth) under a hoodmould. There are transepts each with two east chapels and pilaster buttresses at the corners. The nave has no aisles and is fairly short so lay-brethren cannot ever have formed a large part of this community. Three modern buttresses now prop up the nave south wall, in which is a piscina to serve the lay brothers' altar. The cloister is unusually short from east to west and hardly anything remains of a west range. The east range (now just low walls) contained a chapter house divided by piers into four bays long by three bays wide with three east windows. Between it and the transept was a sacristy, and south of it was a passage, and then a long day-room with just one of its row of columns now remaining. There are traces of the reredorter straddling an open drain at the SE corner and of a building extending east, perhaps an infirmary. The south range has a day-stair in the SE corner, then the warming house with its fireplace and then a long refectory extending southwards. It has three lancets with animal head terminals to the hoodmoulds in the south end wall and two other lancets and a reader's pulpit in the west wall. A hatch connected the refectory with the kitchen in the cloister SW corner.

25

Plan of Grey Abbey

Inch Abbey

INCH ABBEY Co Down J477455 1km N of Downpatrick

In the 1180s John de Courcy founded this abbey for Cistercian monks left homeless by his destruction during the recent wars of their abbey of Carrick at Erenagh 5km to the south, which was originally a Savigniac house founded in 1127. Furness was the mother house. The attractive site at Inch, originally an island in marshes, lies north of the River Quoile, and has remains of a ditch and bank around a large precinct. Only footings remain of the cloister and nothing remains of a western range for lay-brothers but part of the east wall survives of a short refectory extending southwards with a kitchen west of it. There are also remains of the day room in the south end of the east range, which also contained a small chapter house between the sacristy and a small parlour. The lower parts remain of an infirmary to the SE and a bakehouse to the SW. More impressive are the remains of the east part of the church, with triple east lancets and pairs of lancets on each side beyond the pairs of chapels opening out of the transepts. The north transept NW corner has a staircase turret which still stands high. Only footings remain of the aisled nave of five bays with piers more in the nature of short chunks of wall with filleted rolls at the corners and attached shafts. In the 15th century the nave was abandoned, and the church made much more compact by walling up the north and south arches of the crossing and building a new west wall just east of the first set of piers of the nave arcades. The 13th century doorway reset in this new west wall is thought to have once been the main doorway between the church and cloister.

KILLYDONNELL FRIARY Co Donegal C251183 3.5km SW of Ramelton

In the grounds of Fort Stewart are ivy-covered and mostly featureless ruins of a church measuring 24m by 5.8m internally and east and north domestic ranges with vaulted rooms, one of which, on the east, next to the church, now forms a mausoleum. The cloister court is tiny and probably never had proper alleys. Both ranges retain staircases. The church has a south transept with two altar recesses formed in a thick east wall. This Franciscan Third Order friary founded in 1471 by Calvagh O'Donnell was suppressed c1603, when the lands were granted to Captain Basil Brooke. See p28

ULSTER ABBEYS & FRIARIES 27

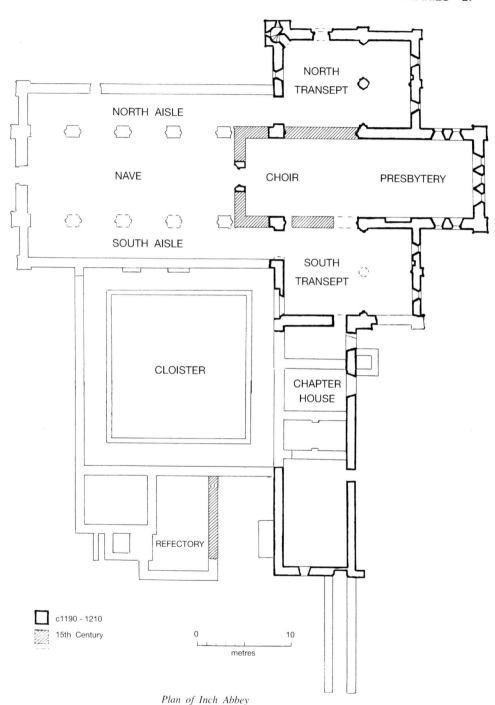

Plan of Inch Abbey

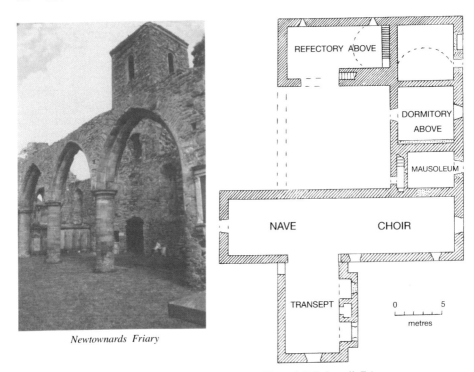

Newtownards Friary

Plan of Killydonnell Friary

KILMACRENAN FRIARY Co Donegal C145207 9km NW of Letterkenny

Magnus O'Donnell founded a Franciscan Third Order friary here c1537, which took over the lands of an Early Christian monastery founded by St Colmcille. The friars were probably dispersed after James I granted the lands to James Fullerton in 1603. Parts remain of an oblong church 25.5m by 6m internally, although no features survive and only the south wall stands high.

LISGOOLE ABBEY Co Fermanagh H240417 2km S of Enniskillen

An altered medieval tower forms part of the north side of an early 19th century villa. St Aid of Lisgovel founded an early monastery here. A new monastery was built in 1106 and c1150 this became an Augustinian priory. In 1485 its dedication was noted as being to St Peter, St Paul and St Mary. By the 1580s both the buildings and the services were neglected by the Augustinian abbot Cahill MacBrian so Cuchonnaght Maguire, lord of Fermanagh made an agreement for the buildings to be restored for use by Franciscan friars. However they were driven out in 1598.

MAGHERABEG FRIARY Co Donegal G925770 2km SSE of Donegal

The remains of a church 6.6m wide by 28.5m long of a Franciscan Third Order friary founded in the 15th century are ivy-covered and of little interest. A blocked doorway leads towards where there is a domestic range, now represented by its fragmentary east wall, with the gap of one former window.

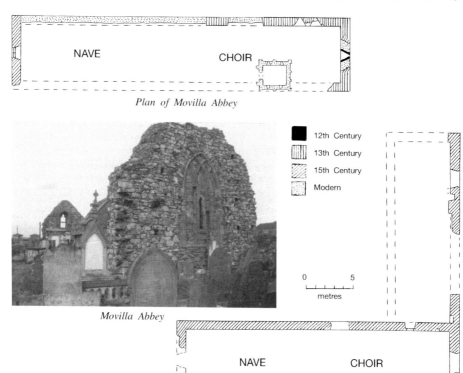

Plan of Movilla Abbey

Movilla Abbey

Plan of Magherabeg Friary

MAGHERAGLASS PRIORY Co Tyrone H743767 West of Cookstown

Featureless ruins survive of an oblong church of an Augustinian priory founded by Terence O'Hagan in 1242. The O'Hagans fortified it in the late 16th century.

MOVILLA ABBEY Co Down J504744 1.5km E of Newtownards

In the 12th century an Augustinian abbey replaced an early monastery possibly founded in the 6th century by St Finnian and plundered by Vikings in 824. Of a church 6m wide and 34m long internally there remain the west wall with a 15th century two-light window with a transom, the late medieval east window once of three lights, with an early window reset in the blocking, and part of the north wall with two lancets. There is a very fine collection of foliated cross-slabs.

NEWTOWNARDS FRIARY Co Down J493738 In town centre

The 13th century nave and 14th century north arcade of four bays remain of the church of a Dominican friary probably founded by the Savage family. In the mid 16th century the Clannaboy O'Neills destroyed the buildings to prevent them holding an English garrison. The church was restored for Protestant use in 1632-6 by the 1st Viscount Montgomery, when a tower was added on the north side of the aisle. There are memorials to the Londonderry and Colville families, who succeeded the Montgomerys.

RATHMULLAN FRIARY Co Donegal C296275 18km NW of Derry

This Camelite friary of St Mary is said to have been founded in 1403, although the earliest features are remains of mid 15th century windows of three and two lights in the east and south walls of the choir of the church, which is 27.5m long by 6.3m wide internally. The central tower with its two narrow arches probably dates from 1516, when the friary was refounded by the MacSweenys of Fanad. It has a staircase turret on the south side. In 1595 the friary was plundered by an English naval force under George Bingham but the friars seem to have returned until the friary was granted to Sir James Fullerton c1603. He assigned the buildings to Sir Ralph Bingley to use as a barracks.

Andrew Knox, Protestant Bishop of Raphoe obtained the friary c1617 and converted the nave and south transept into an L-shaped fortified house, now largely ivy-covered and with most of its windows blocked up. Circular bartizans with moulded corbelled courses of the type then usual in Scottish houses were added to the western corners of the nave, which was remodelled to contain two main storeys and an attic in the roof. A turret bearing the date 1618, and having a machicolation over the new entrance doorway onto the foot of a wooden scale-and-platt staircase, was built within the angle between the nave and the transept, which then contained three full storeys, the lowest perhaps a kitchen. Mullioned windows replaced recesses for altars in the transept east wall. The choir remained as a private chapel and is said to have later served as a parish church until 1814, although it seems rather small on its own for that purpose. Only the east wall with a pair of two-light windows and the north end wall remain of the east range of the claustral buildings. An English campaign map of 1599 suggests that a north range also once existed. Where the cloister would have been is now divided in two by a modern wall.

Rathmullan Friary

Killydonnell Friary

ULSTER ABBEYS & FRIARIES   31

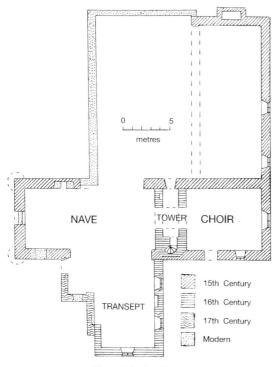

Plan of Rathmullen Friary   *Rathmullan Friary*

TIVEA LOUGH FRIARY   Co Fermanagh   G978598   By lough 4km E of Belleek
An oblong church with a thin cusped east lancet by the shore of Keenaghan Lough is said to have once been used by the Franciscans.

OTHER MEDIEVAL MONASTIC SITES IN ULSTER

CARRICKFERGUS Co Antrim Joymount House lies on the site of a Franciscan friary
   founded in 1248 which became Observant in 1497. It later served as a store.
COMBER Co Down J461692 Church on site of Cistercian abbey founded c1200.
HOLLYWOOD   Co Down J477455 Small church later used by Franciscan friars.
TEMPLE DOUGLAS Co Donegal Oblong church with plate tracery in east window.
TRINITY Co Cavan H352042 12th century church later used by Premonstratensians
      17th century transept. Probable source of Romanesque doorway now at Kilmore.
The Augustinians had priories at Armagh, Clogher (Tyrone), Kells (near Connor) and
      Muckamore (SE of Antrim), A tomb remains of the priory at Saul (J510463). The
      Augustinians also had friaries at Derry and beside Lough Derg.
The Cistercians had abbeys at Kilmonaster, Newry and a nunnery at Downpatrick.
The Franciscans had friaries at Cavan (H420048), Clonosey (H389163), Killybegs,
      Lambeg (J275666), Monaghan, Omagh, Rossnowlagh & probably Derry and Inver.
The Dominicans had a friary at Coleraine and the Premonstratensians had a priory at Carrickfergus. Early monasteries at Killevy (a nunnery), Nendrum, and Tory Island survived until the 16th century. All retain fragmentary remains of ancient churches.

MUNSTER ABBEYS AND FRIARIES

ABBEYDORNEY ABBEY Co Kerry Q850232 9km N of Tralee

This was supposedly a Cistercian abbey colonised from Monasteranenagh in 1154. The remains appear to be entirely 15th century and look more like a friary, having a plain oblong church with a thin tower-like structure at the west end, where the entrance doorway is located. The east window has sub-arches and smaller windows are round-headed. To the south are remains of claustral buildings choked with graves and there are fragments of former cloister arcade piers of a late medieval dumb-bell type. Here in 1186 died Gillachrist O'Conachy, first Abbot of Mellifont and later Bishop of Lismore and Papal Legate.

ADARE PRIORY Co Limerick R464462 In the middle of the village of Adare

The monastery of Trinitarian Canons of the Order of the Redemption of Captives, the only one of its type known in Ireland, is said to have been founded in 1230 and enlarged in 1275. The church was originally dedicated to St James but now forms part of a Catholic church of Holy Trinity. In 1852 the 3rd Earl of Dunraven had a porch and west extension added to the nave, battlements and turrets added to the vaulted central tower, and the short choir rebuilt. A few years later a new nave and north aisle were added, so that the original nave, which has original blank arcading on its south side, has now become a south aisle. No medieval windows survive. The new nave and aisle fill part of the space of the former cloister. A building still in use as a convent school to the NW of the church is one of the old claustal buildings renovated and heightened.

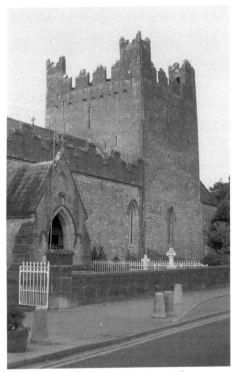

Trinitarian Priory church at Adare

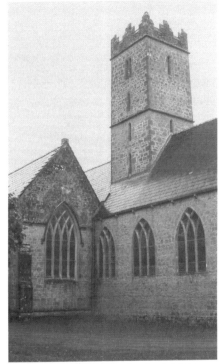

Augustinian Friary church at Adare

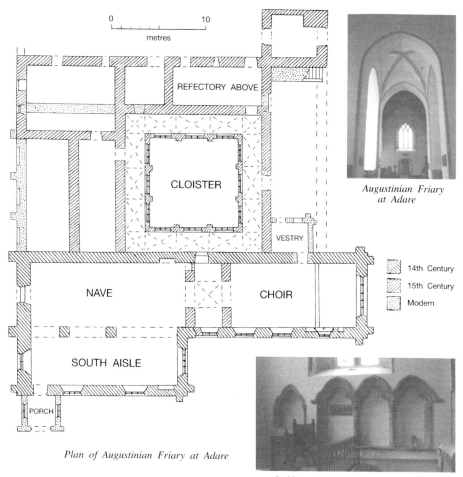

Plan of Augustinian Friary at Adare

Sedilia at Augustinian Friary at Adare

ADARE FRIARY   Co Limerick   R469466   0.4km NE of Adare village

On the south bank of the River Maigue is an Augustinian friary founded by Thomas FitzGerald, Lord Offaly about the time when he was made 1st Earl of Kildare in 1316. In 1807-14 the church was restored by the Ecclesiastical Commissioners for Protestant worship, when the 15th century parapets of the 14th century choir were removed. The choir still has some good 14th century windows and sedilia. Other windows with intersecting tracery survive in the aisle, which has an arcade of three unequal sized arches and set-back buttresses like those of the choir. Of the 15th century are the central tower, the ogival-headed tomb recess with crocketed pinnacles, and the cloister with rows of three-light windows set on the north side towards the river (which thus drained the latrines), The north and east alleys of the cloister were partly rebuilt in 1831 by the 2nd Earl of Dunraven. The alleys are all vaulted. Not much remains of the former east range but the north range retains a series of vaults and an upper room which was re-roofed in 1814 to serve as a school. Other buildings of the 1850s extend to the NE.

Franciscan Friary at Adare

ADARE FRIARY   Co Limerick   R474467   1km NE of Adare village

The Observant Franciscan friary founded in 1464 by Thomas FitzGerald, 7th Earl of Kildare and his wife Johanna, daughter of the Earl of Desmond, now isolated in the middle of a golf course, has one of the most extensive sets of monastic buildings now surviving in Ireland, partly as a result of some restoration in 1875 by the antiquarian Earl of Dunraven. A detailed list of benefactors dating from the 17th century tells us that the founders built the nave and choir of the church, providing their windows with stained glass, and one side of the cloister. The unusually thin central tower set on arches between the nave and choir was added at the expense of Cornelius O'Sullivan, who died in 1492. Donogh O'Brien paid for the dormitory, Morough O'Hickey provided the refectory and Edmund FitzGerald, Knight of Glin and his wife Honoria O'Mahony contributed the infirmary (all probably in the 1480s and 90s), while several others provided other parts of the cloister and several additional chapels. One of these chapels unusually forms a SW projection from the western aisle of the south transept built c1475-80 at the expense of Margaret FitzGibbon. Two other chapels fitted with shallow tomb recesses with ogival arches with finials and crocketed pinnacles project from the transept east wall, the northern chapel being largest with two tomb recesses on each side. An arcade of two bays divides the nave from the transept and the arcade between the transept and its aisle has rectangular piers between three arches and a fourth which is no wider than a doorway. The choir has a four-light east window, set-back corner buttresses and four south windows each of two lights. The southern lower room of the east range adjoins the choir north wall and served as a sacristy. At the north end of this range is a latrine block. It formed part of the east side of a second court enclosed by more ruinous service buildings. Buttresses divide each side of the cloister arcade into bays each with a window of three lights, although there is an inconsistency of design resulting from the different contributions made by different patrons.

MUNSTER ABBEYS & FRIARIES 35

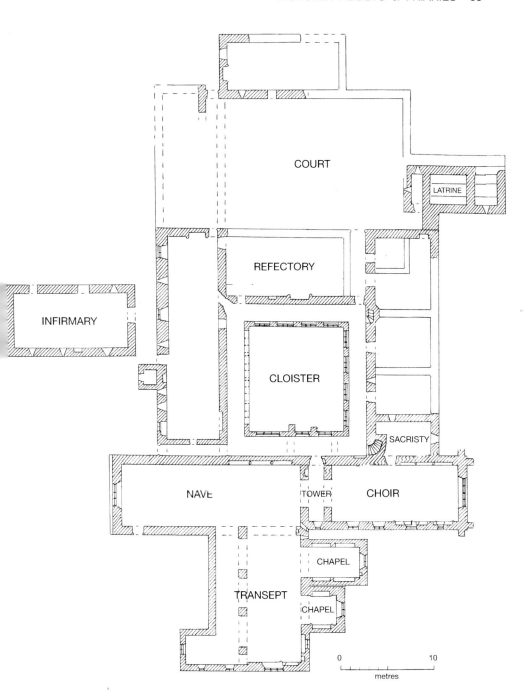

Plan of Franciscan Friary at Adare

36   MUNSTER ABBEYS AND FRIARIES

The cloister at Ardfert Friary

Church of Ainy Preceptory

AINY PRECEPTORY   Co Limerick   R706361   Beside church at N end of Hospital

Ainy was the second most important preceptory of the Knights Hospitaller in Ireland. Of it there remain a 13th century church with several lancets and an original doorway. A grotto has been formed in the upper level of a two storey residential west end. Inside are three tombs with effigies of mid 13th to 14th descendants of Geoffrey de Marisco, the English Justiciar, who founded the preceptory shortly before 1215.

ARDFERT FRIARY   Co Kerry   Q791212   To E of Ardfert, 8km NW of Ardfert

Thomas FitzMaurice, Baron of Kerry founded this Franciscan Friary in 1253. The friars became Observant in 1518. In the late 16th century the friary became a barracks but was later taken over by a Protestant bishop who is thought to have held services in the choir. Original 13th century features are the five stepped lancets in the east wall of the choir and the continuous row of nine lancets on the south side. The south aisle with its arcade of round piers is 14th century. The south transept with its fine end window and tomb-recesses, the unusual western tower and the cloister and its surviving eastern dormitory range are 15th century. The cloister seems to be of c1470 and has triple arches under segmental-pointed arches set on larger piers. There is evidence at the SW corner that the alleys had lean-to roofs formed of overlapping stone tiles.

ARDFINNAN FRIARY   Co Tipperary   S072164   1km SW of Ardfinnan

The Carmelite friary of Lady's Abbey at Monroe near Ardfinnan has a 16th century church which is 28.8m long by 7m wide internally. A tower is placed further west than usual, resulting in a short nave. The choir has a two-light east window and two north doorways, the eastern of which opened into a sacristy. There is no direct communication with a chapel with a pair of two-light windows on the south side.

Tower of Askeaton Priory

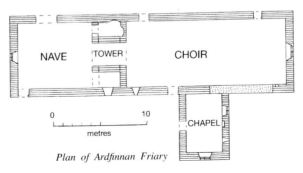
Plan of Ardfinnan Friary

MUNSTER ABBEYS & FRIARIES

Ardfert Friary

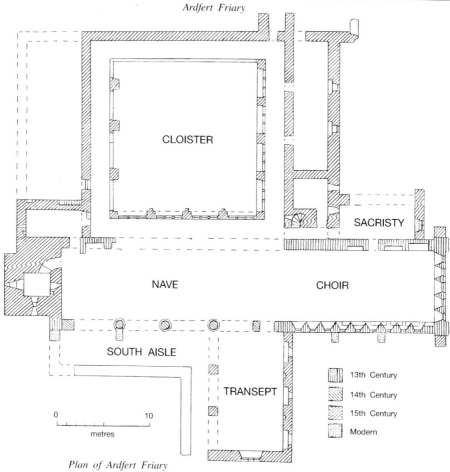

Plan of Ardfert Friary

ASKEATON FRIARY Co Limerick   R340507   To N of town of Askeaton

This Franciscan friary on the east bank of the Fiver Deel became Observant in 1490 and is unusual for a friary of its period in having the well-preserved cloister on the south side, where it was easier to provide drainage for latrines and a water supply. Several friars were killed when Sir John Malbie plundered the friary during his unsuccessful attack on the nearby castle in 1579. The friary was re-occupied in 1627 and friars are said to have at least occasionally used it as late as 1714. The buildings are remarkably complete apart from the loss of the NW corner of the north transept and the west wall of the sacristy north of the choir, where a tower once adjoined. Both the lost parts may have been destroyed during the wars of 1642-52.

Gerald, 4th Earl of Desmond is said to have founded this friary in 1389 but the church and claustral buildings appear to be mostly of c1420-40 and the refectory range extending south from the cloister is probably an addition of the 1460s or 70s, modifying the original plan. The refectory has a reader's pulpit. The church has windows with intersecting tracery, of five lights in the east wall and of three lights elsewhere. One on the south side set over the sedilia has cusps to the sides of the main lights. The only really different window is one of two lights with tracery on the north side, roughly where the screen and pulpitum are assumed to have stood. Three tomb niches of c1470-90 on the south and one on the north further east have ogival hoods with finials and pilasters with crocketed pinnacles. The east and west ranges of the claustral buildings are narrow at ground level but the upper storey lies over the cloister alleys to give greater width. St Francis with a Stigmata is depicted at the NE corner of the cloister arcades. The buildings are currently entered at the SE corner, where there is a spiral staircase and the church itself has no external doorways apart from one now blocked at the north end of the three bay western aisle of the north transept. This transept is a late 15th century addition and has a two bay arcade towards the nave and one remaining out of an original series of three altar niches in the east wall.

Askeaton Franciscan Friary

Refectory at Askeaton Franciscan Friary

MUNSTER ABBEYS & FRIARIES 39

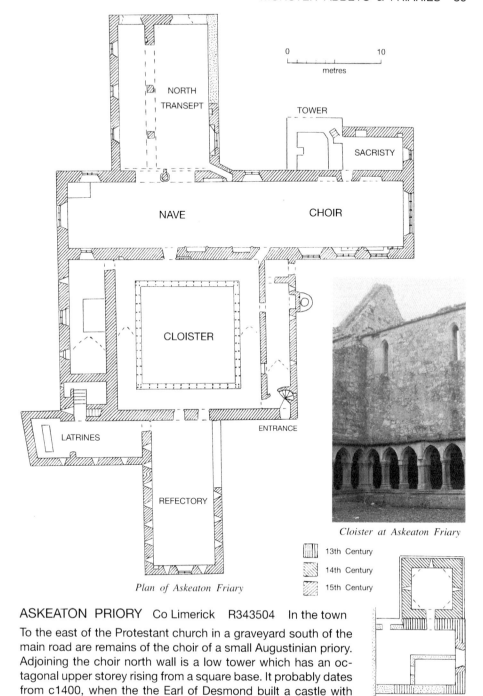

Cloister at Askeaton Friary

Plan of Askeaton Friary

Askeaton Priory: plan

ASKEATON PRIORY Co Limerick R343504 In the town
To the east of the Protestant church in a graveyard south of the main road are remains of the choir of a small Augustinian priory. Adjoining the choir north wall is a low tower which has an octagonal upper storey rising from a square base. It probably dates from c1400, when the the Earl of Desmond built a castle with two big octagonal towers at Glenogra further east in Limerick.

ATHASSEL PRIORY   Co Tipperary

William FitzAdelm de Burgh founded this Augustinian priory dedicated to St Edmund in the 1190s. An aggressive conqueror, he is said to have been buried here in 1205, as were his son and grandson. The monastery was large and important enough for the prior to be entitled to a seat in medieval parliaments. The large aisled nave of six bays probably built in the 1270s at the expense of William de Burgh, Earl of Ulster seems to have been abandoned after the priory was attacked and burned in 1447 and its arcades have gone. The attack seems to have ended the glory days of the priory. In the 1550s Queen Mary granted it to Thomas, Earl of Ormond.

The church was 61m long internally and had a heavily-buttressed bell-tower at the NW corner. The eastern parts of the church probably date from the 1220s or 30s and comprise transepts with eastern chapels and a choir with a row of four lancets (originally five) on each side. The east window is 15th century, when the north and south arches of the crossing were blocked up with solid walls to support a new tower replacing an older one, but the screen wall containing windows flanking a fine doorway of four orders with roll-mouldings under the west arch is probably of c1260. A recess above it must have held a rood. The north aisle has buttresses and remains of two-light windows and wall-shafts, and there was a wide west doorway. The large building adjoining the northernmost chapel was probably an early 14th century Lady Chapel.

Two thirds of the 15th century cloister arcades remain, with triplets of lancets between buttresses, and the domestic buildings are unusually complete. On the west side is a vaulted outer parlour and a cellar. On the south are vaulted cellars that supported the refectory. The east range has a row of six equal-sized vaulted rooms under the dormitory. The first three were a sacristy, a passage and an ante-room for a chapter house set beyond the range. At the SE corner are latrines over a drain. To the east, south and west a precinct wall encloses four acres, the entrance on the west being over a moat by means of a bridge and then through a gatehouse. There are remains of various outbuildings, including what is probably the infirmary to the SW.

Athassel Priory from the west

MUNSTER ABBEYS & FRIARIES

Doorway into the choir at Athassel

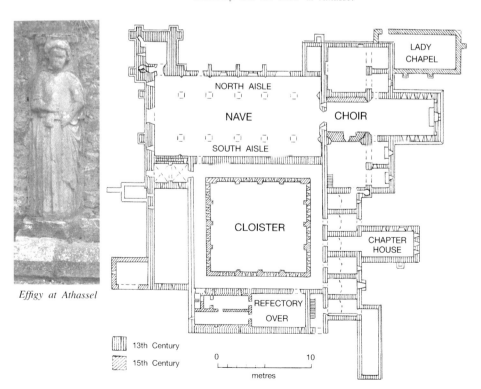

Effigy at Athassel

Plan of Athassel Priory

42   MUNSTER ABBEYS AND FRIARIES

Ballybeg Priory

Ballinskelligs Priory

BALLINSKELLIGS PRIORY   Co Kerry   V434650   14km SSW of Cahersiveen

The monks from the remote offshore monastery of Skellig Michael are said to have moved here at the turn of the 12th and 13th centuries and to have adopted the Augustinian rule, again dedicating their church to St Michael. A narrow plain pointed arch not likely to later than c1220 connected a narrow nave with several lancets and north and south doorways to a wider choir, most of which has been lost to the sea. There appears to have been a small cloister on the south side of the nave and beyond it are remains of a range which probably formed a refectory. It has two late medieval windows. Fragments of other buildings lie further to the south. Adjoining the nave NW corner is a building of uncertain date with a late medieval upper two-light east window. After suppression the buildings were held in turn by the Hardings and the Sigersons.

BALLYBEG PRIORY   Co Cork   W543077   1km S of Buttevant

The Augustinian priory of St Thomas founded by Philip de Barry in 1229 had a church 50m long by 8m wide internally. A high fragment remains of the SE corner where there are traces of sedilia. The west end also survives with two 13th century lancets. This part was later incorporated into a tower and remained in use as part of farmbuildings until the early 20th century. Two doorways in the south wall open towards a cloister 25m square with low walls marking its garth. The cloister is set so that it extends somewhat further west than the church, its north side being bounded by a much rebuilt wall. Little remains of the outer walls of the ranges around the cloister but the base of a fine chapter house doorway can be seen on the east and on the south side there are traces of the refectory pulpit staircase and a vaulted passage leading south from the cloister SE corner. In the late medieval period a four storey tower was added to the north end of the west range. The second storey is vaulted and there are mural chambers over the entrance and lower staircase in the east wall. The upper storeys are linked by a spiral staircase in the SE corner. The fourth storey has a two-light window. North of the church is the lower part of a late medieval tower house and to the SE lies a circular dovecot with 350 nesting boxes and an upper doorway that may have been reached from a wall-walk on the top of an adjacent section of a precinct wall.

MUNSTER ABBEYS & FRIARIES   43

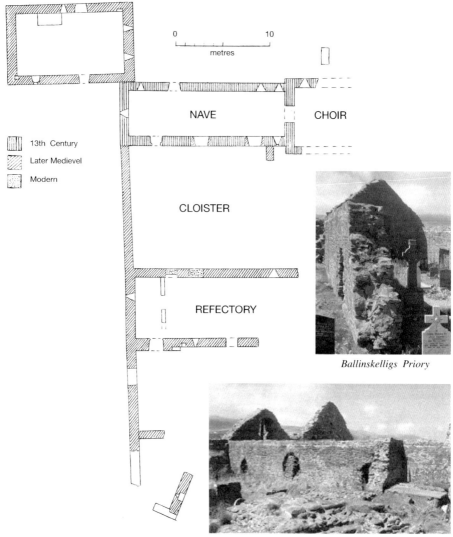

Plan of Ballinskelligs Priory   *Ballinskelligs Priory*

BALLYMACADANE ABBEY   Co Cork   W608652   10km SW of Cork

This fragmentary church 26m long by 6m wide internally is thought to have originally served a convent of Augustinian nuns founded by Cormac MacCarthy in the late 15th century. It seems to have been used by Franciscan friars for a while after the suppression. Not much remains of the east window but a piscina remains below a two-light window on the south side and the north wall contains two doorways. One led to a NE sacristy. The other seems to have connected a cloister with a space under a central tower, the north piers of which remain.

Bridgetown Priory from the south

BRIDGETOWN PRIORY   Co Cork   W692998   2.5km SSE of Castletownroche

Alexander FitzHugh founded this Augustinian priory in the early 13th century. Recently the ruins have been stripped of ivy and repointed. A gabled wall with a narrow central arch and two upper windows divides a 23m long nave from a 25m long choir with corner buttresses. Both are 7.8m wide and have original lancets. Of c1300 is a window on the south side of the choir and probably the tomb niches of later patrons, the Roches. There were three east lancets but a late medieval two-light window has replaced the middle one. Also late medieval are the three storey turret set on the choir NE corner, the Lady Chapel on the south side, and the low gabled tower set within the west end of the nave with two vaulted rooms in its lowest level. A spiral staircase in a turret at the NE corner connects the upper levels, which were partly rebuilt in the 17th century.

Just east of the tower the nave has opposed north and south doorways, the latter towards a cloister 23m across with the east alley partly vaulted. There is just a blind high wall on the west. On the south is a block with three cellars later subdivided by arches and piers, above which is a refectory with a row of eight south-facing lancets and one jamb of a reader's pulpit. In the west gable are later gunloops. The east range is irregularly set and has a central chapter house with three east lancets and other rooms on either side, the dooways all being later medieval. South of this range was a square kitchen and to the east is a court 18m square, on the south side of which are rooms for the prior converted from what was once either an infirmary or a large latrine block. The lodging has a small tower on the south side. Its SE corner leans as a result of unstable ground.

The west end of Buttevant Friary

Old print of Buttevant Friary

BUTTEVANT FRIARY Co Cork   R543090   In middle of Buttevant

The church measuring 46m by 7.5m internally must have been built immediately after David Barry founded this Franciscan friary dedicated to St Thomas Becket in 1251. The nave has two rounded multi-foiled tomb recesses and several original lancets, including two in the west wall wide enough to each have late-medieval windows of two ogival-headed lights inserted into them. The doorway below these windows is also late medieval. A row of eight lancets remains in the choir south wall, two of them now blocked up and others replaced by late medieval windows of three lights. Ogival heads have been inserted into the triple east lancets. Under the east end of the choir is a crypt with two levels of small chambers with late medieval vaults, the upper level having an older quatrefoil-shaped pier with stiff-leaf foliage on the capitals. Little remains of the central tower, which collapsed c1820, but old illustrations of it showing banded angle-shafts suggest it had been added by 1300.

Lancets in the south wall show that the south transept had also been added by 1300. Buttressing added to the corners has partly obliterated two of the south lancets and also lancets facing east and west. The east chapel with a tomb-recess inserted in its east window is a later addition. Of a cloister to the north there remain only corbels and part of the west wall of the east range. These buildings were repaired in 1604 and used during much of the 17th century. The six storey late medieval tower set between the nave and transept of the modern Catholic church to the NW is thought to have formed part of precinct defences added possibly after one of the earls of Desmond retired here. The Barrys took possession after suppression and ignored their undertaking not to let the friars return. In the end friars remained here intermittantly until 1783.

46 MUNSTER ABBEYS AND FRIARIES

CAHIR PRIORY Co Tipperary S049253 On west bank of Suir to north of castle
Geoffrey de Camville founded this Augustinian priory c1220. Rows of original lancets still remain in the north wall of the choir and in the south wall of the refectory on the south side of a cloister 21.5m square on the south side. Only the south wall with a later doorway remains of the nave. The choir has a single south lancet and later medieval windows on all three sides at the east end. The buildings were much altered in the 15th century and again in the late 16th century after the suppression when the choir and the eastern range appear to have been adapted as a mansion. A tower with a spiral staircase in a projecting NW turret lying between the nave and chancel has late Tudor type upper windows probably of c1580-1600 and presumably later insertions. Crosswalls and vaults have been inserted in the east range and part of the south range adjoining it forms a second smaller tower.

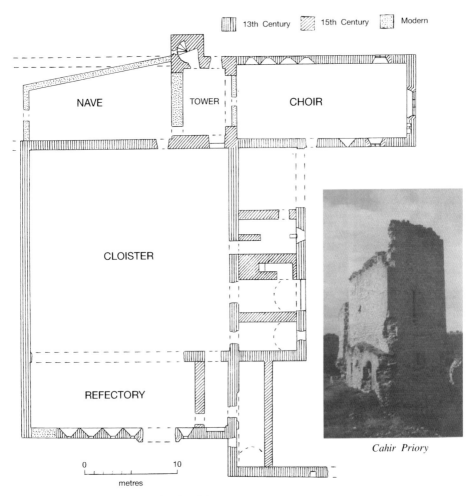

Cahir Priory

Plan of Cahir Priory

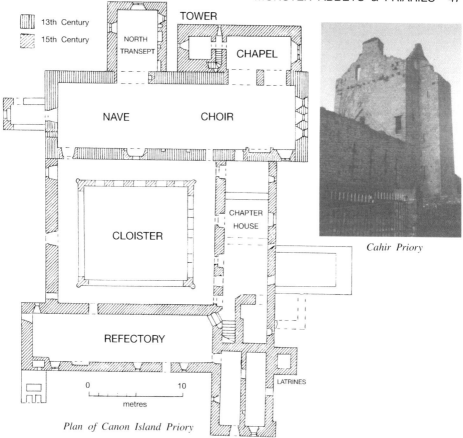

Cahir Priory

Plan of Canon Island Priory

CANON ISLAND PRIORY   Co Clare   R299591   20km SSW of Ennis

The 13th century church of this Augustinian priory of St Mary on an island in the Shannon estuary has three east lancets and measures 25m by 7m. In the 15th century a transept with two-light windows and tower were added on the north side, with a chapel with a two bay arcade east of the latter. The chapel has a three-light east window. A small cloister was also added, with east and south domestic ranges, the latter containing a kitchen and refectory. A latrine turret projects east beside the southern part of the east range, which has two parallel vaults running north-south. The northern part of this range, now lacking its crosswalls, may be remodelled 13th century work. The northern alley of the cloister preserves its arcade, and the other two corners also remain. In 1543 the priory reverted to its founders, the O'Briens, and was held by them until Henry, 7th Earl of Thomond granted it to Richard Henn in 1712.

CARRICKMAGRIFFIN FRIARY   Co Tipperary   S398216   Carrigbeg, S of R. Suir

The Catholic church of St Molleran daringly built in 1827 before Emancipation incorporates part of the north wall with a corbelled bell-turret of the church of a Franciscan friary of St Michael founded in 1336 by James, 1st Earl of Ormond. Fresh domestic buildings seem to have been begun in the 1440s with Eamon MacRisderd as patron.

48 MUNSTER ABBEYS AND FRIARIES

Cashel Dominican Friary

Castlelyons Friary

CASHEL FRIARY   Co Tipperary   S077407   In Moor Lane, off Main Street

A row of nine 13th century lancets (some headless or blocked) remain in the choir of the church of a Dominican friary founded in 1243 by Archbishop David MacKelly. Other windows with flowing tracery and an oblong central tower were inserted by Archbishop John Cantwell in 1480 following an accidental fire, but the south transept may be late 13th century. General Chapters of the order were held here in 1289 and 1307. See p3

CASHEL FRIARY   Co Tipperary   S079405   In churchyard in Friar Street

All that remains of the once-important Franciscan friary founded by Archbishop Hackett c1265 is part of a 14th century military effigy and a tomb chest now used as a stoup in the porch of the church of St John the Baptist.

CASTLELYONS FRIARY   Co Cork   W840930   On W side of village

John de Barry founded this Carmelite friary in 1307 but the existing remains appear to be all late medieval. The church measures 43.5m by 7.5m internally and has a central tower which is wider than usual. The nave is fairly complete, with a good west doorway surmounted by a two-light window, although the gable on top has gone. Most of the north and east walls of the tower have fallen, but the other walls still stand three storeys high with a wall-walk and parapet, the staircase in the NW corner is complete, and parts remain of the groin-vault. The choir south wall fell in 1871 and the NW corner is the only part now standing more than a metre high, with a jamb of a large east window. There are many worn cross-slabs. A doorway under the tower leads to a cloister with some remains to the south and there are fairly complete east and west ranges each having a latrine shute on a southern corner serving the dormitories. The east range has a west fireplace on the lower level. The west dormitory is reached from the cloister by a spiral stair in the nave south wall. The south range has gone. Friars of one kind or another remained in the locality for many years and the last titular prior died in 1760.

MUNSTER ABBEYS & FRIARIES 49

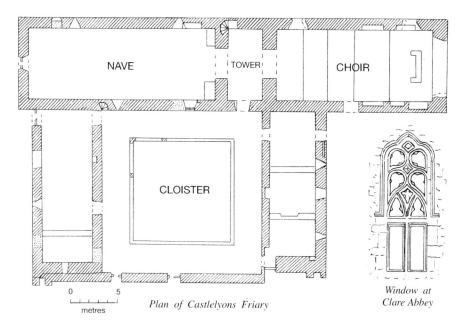

Plan of Castlelyons Friary

Window at Clare Abbey

CLARE ABBEY Co Clare   R348758   2km SSE of Ennis

This Augustinian priory dedicated to St Peter and St Paul was founded in 1189 by Donal Mor O'Brien. In 1278 it was the scene of a battle between different branches of the O'Brien family. Parts of the church may go back to the 1190s but the east window and central tower probably date from just after 1461, when Teige Acomhad O'Brien granted the abbey a new charter. The 25m square cloister and its south and east ranges are also of that period. The gable at the end of the east range contains a window of very unusual form with trefoiled heads just above a mullion and two pairs of mouchettes above. This can hardly have been the window of a dormitory. Either the room behind it served some other purpose such as a scriptorium, or the window has been moved, or it is a post-suppression insertion. The priory officially reverted to the O'Briens in 1541, but the canons seem to have remained in residence until Cromwellian times. See p6.

CLONMEL FRIARY   Co Tipperary   S205223   In Abbey St, in SE part of town

The Franciscan friary church of 1884-6 incorporates the unusually substantial 15th century central tower and the 13th century north wall of the choir of the medieval friary founded in 1269 by the de Grandison family, who had just taken control of Clonmel. The buildings became part of a Cromwellian fort in the 1650s. In the 1820s the friars finally regained possession of the site.

CORBALLY PRIORY   Co Tipperary   S153885   2km SSE of Roscrea

In the 1480s the Augustinian community at Monaincha moved to Corbally nearby and added north and south transepts to an older church also known as Sean Ross. The south transept has a squint towards the main altar and the end window has ogival-headed lights and a transom, whilst the north transept end window had flowing tracery. The ruins are very overgrown and little can now be seen of the nave.

The presbytery at Corcomroe Abbey

Effigy at Corcomroe Abbey

Capitals at Corcomroe Abbey

CORCOMROE ABBEY Co Clare M295090 6km ENE of Ballyvaghan

In the 1190s Donal O'Brien had a colony of Cistercian monks sent over from Inishlounaght in Tipperary to found this abbey of St Mary. The eastern part of the church is of c1200, finely executed although on a modest scale, since the transepts were no more than lean-to roofed continuations of the aisles, each with just a single barrel-vaulted east chapel. The presbytery is vaulted in two bays and has three east lancets and a pair of sedilia on the north side, next to a tomb-recess with a crude effigy of Conor na Siudaine O'Brien, d1267. Above is a figure of a late medieval abbot. The crossing arches are pointed and have capitals carved with leaves, acorns and a lotus plant. The arch into the south chapel has capitals with human masks. Also of c1200 is the range east of the small cloister, with a modest chapter house with two east lancets. There are no other remains of claustral ranges, but there is an infirmary or guesthouse to the south and part of a gatehouse which collapsed in 1840 to the west.

Of the 13th century are the west wall of the cloister with its doorway, the south aisle of the church and the western part of the nave with arcades of two pointed arches on the south side and three on the north. Two of the northern arches have been blocked up, for in the 15th century this part of the church was walled off and probably used for domestic purposes. The blocking wall supported a turret and has a central doorway with a drawbar slot. There is another in the west wall of the north transept, towards the former north aisle then abandoned.

The abbey became subject to that of Furness in Lancashire in 1295. Dermot O'Brien used it as a headquarters after the battle of Drom Lurgan in 1317. The abbey reverted to the O'Briens after suppression and went to Richard Harding in 1611, although a few monks seem to have remained into that period as there is a record of a new abbot, John O'Dea, being appointed in 1628.

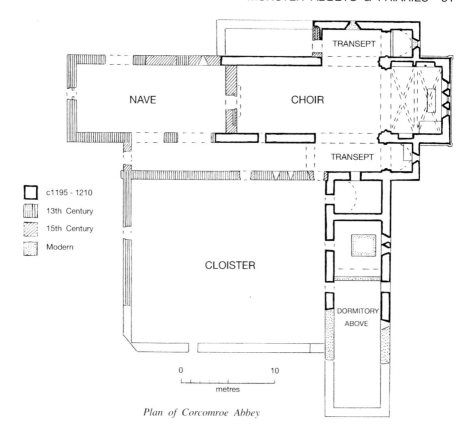

Plan of Corcomroe Abbey

CORK FRIARY Co Cork W675713 On north side of Red Abbey Street.

Only the rectangular central tower now remains of an Augustinian friary founded in the late 13th century and said to have remained in use by friars until the 1640s, although officially dissolved in 1541, when there is a mention of chapels, a dormitory, and a hall and buttery. Considerably more still remained of the church in 1873. The tower has a barrel-vault, water spouts and a top storey which is reduced to a square.

Nearby is the site of the Augustinian Gill Abbey, founded by Cormac MacCarthy c1136, and named after the first abbot, Gilla Aedha O'Muidhin.

Nothing now remains standing of the Franciscan and Dominican friaries of Cork, supposedly both founded in 1229. The latter was dedicated to St Mary and lay on an island west of the city. Excavations have revealed traces of the cloister and church and a few loose carved fragments remain at a private house in Boreenmanagh Road.

CROOKE PRECEPTORY Co Waterford X697089 1.5km SSW of Passage East

An east gable with three lancets robbed of dressed stones and wall-footings remain of a church 25m long which originally belonged to a preceptory of the Knights Templars, passing to the Knights Hospitallers in 1327. By 1541 it was probably in use as a parish church and it was still in good repair in 1613. A castle lies just 70m to the south.

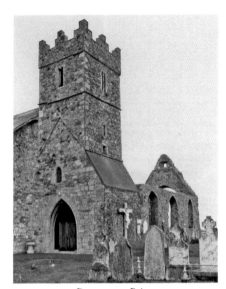

Ennis Friary   *Dungarvan Priory*

DUNGARVAN PRIORY   Co Waterford   X267929   At Abbeyside E of the estuary

Of the Augustinian priory founded c1290 by Thomas FitzMaurice FitzGerald there remain the choir and central tower, the latter still in use to serve an adjoining modern Augustinian church extending to the north on the side of a former transept. The choir has remains of three wide windows in the south wall whilst the east window was probably of four lights.

ENNIS FRIARY   Co Clare   R339777   Towards N end of town centre

Founded c1240 by Donachad Cairbreach O'Brien for Franciscans, this friary has a choir with an east window of five lancets of c1290 once filled with blue stained glass donated by Donachad's successor Turlough. The middle three lancets are grouped and separated only by slender mullions. Early in the 14th century Maccon MacNamara provided a new vaulted sacristy on the north side of the choir and also a refectory which has gone. Of the late 15th century are the nave west doorway facing the street and the central tower with a screen showing a bishop and the Virgin and Child under the south arch and a figure of St Francis with the stigmata on the SW pier. The transept windows are also of that period, and also a tomb chest in the choir which has side panels carved with scenes of the Arrest of Christ, the Scourging, the Crucifixion, Christ laid in the tomb, the Resurrection and a panel showing a female of the O'Brien family.

     In the late 14th century the friary had a large number of friars and a flourishing school. It was reformed in 1550, having survived under protection of Murrogh O'Brien, 1st Earl of Thomond, and having the last college of Catholic theology to survive the Reformation. In 1606 the friary was the scene of the formal abolition of the old Irish Brehon laws. It became a parish church in 1615 and the last friar died two years later. A small colony of friars returned in 1628. They were thrown out by the Cromwellians but returned in the 1660s, and the south transept was still roofed in 1681. Deserted by 1700, the friary was formally handed back into Franciscan guardianship in 1969.

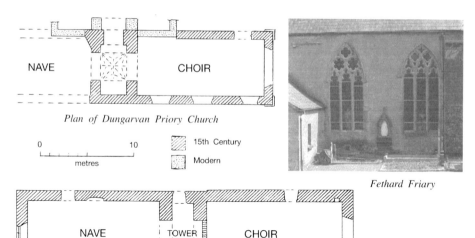

Plan of Dungarvan Priory Church

Fethard Friary

Plan of Glanworth Friary Church

FERMOY ABBEY Co Cork W810984   On S bank of Blackwater at Fermoy

A pointed archway moved to a property boundary on the north side of McCurtain Street and a font in the Protestant church are possible relics of a Cistercian abbey founded in 1170 by Donal Mor O'Brien. In 1227 the monks here were the leaders of the so-called Mellifont Conspiracy in defying the the Cistercian General Chapter. At least part of the church remained in use for Protestant worship after suppression c1540, but all the standing remains were demolished for their materials n 1804.

FETHARD FRIARY Co Tipperary S211349   At E end of walled town

The church of this Augustinian friary has two good Decorated style three-light windows of c1320-40 on the north side of the choir. It was founded c1306 by Walter de Mulcote. The north vestry dates only from when the friars returned and restored the church in the early 19th century. Fragments remain of a former north transept. There are also remains of domestic ranges on the south with a refectory, kitchen and domitory. In a wall near the east end of the church is a sheela-na-gig.

GLANWORTH FRIARY Co Cork W756044   Just N of Glanworth village

The Dominican friary of the Holy Cross was founded by the Roche family c1475. The choir was probably built immediately and the central tower and nave shortly afterwards. The east window with intersecting tracery over four round-arched lights and a hoodmould has been recently returned from the C of I church nearby. Other choir windows of pairs of ogival-headed lights with recessed spandrels under hoodmoulds have been largely robbed of their cut stones but a piscina remains. The tower has four storeys, the second storey room having doorways to wall-walks on the choir. The choir north wall has corbels and a string course for the roof of an adjacent cloister alley. The cloister and the dormitory and hall mentioned in a report of 1541 were demolished in the 19th century to provide materials for building the adjacent road.

Interior of Holy Cross Abbey

Cloister at Holy Cross Abbey

HOLY CROSS ABBEY   Co Tipperary   S090542   6km SW of Thurles

Donal Mor O'Brien founded this abbey for Cistercian monks from Monasteranenagh in 1180, possibly on the site of a short-lived Benedictine priory founded in 1169. A reconstructed late 12th century doorway remains between the south aisle and the cloister. The rest of this aisle and the four western bays of the nave flanked by pointed arches on square piers and containing the lay brothers' choir are 13th century. The abbey had a relic of the True Cross which brought in many pilgrims and the wealth thus generated allowed the total rebuilding c1450-75 of the rest of the church (re-roofed in 1971-5) and the domestic buildings. The original plan was retained with the monks' choir in the eastern part of the nave, transepts each with two eastern chapels, a central tower and a short embattled presbytery with heavy corner buttresses to help support the rib-vaults. The six-light east window has reticulated tracery. The sedilia on the south side have the arms of the Earls of Ormond and the English Crown in blind arcading with crocketed finials and pinnacles above, and a projecting canopy on top. There are many two and three light windows around the church displaying various forms of Flamboyant tracery. In the north transept are wall-paintings (a rarity in Ireland) showing a deer being hunted by men with bows and a dog on a lead. The so-called "Monks Waking Place" with columns and arches between the two south chapels was a shrine housing the relic of the Cross said to have been given by Pope Paschal II to Muirchertach O'Brien c1110. The night stair from the dormitory survives in the south transept.

Parts of the cloister arcades were re-erected in 1928. Not much remains of the refectory along the south side but the east and west ranges are still complete, with a sacristy between the south transept and a chapter house with a fine entrance doorway in the east range. A latrine block once extended east from the south end of the dormitory to link up with the infirmary complex, of which there are substantial ruins. Extending south from the site of the latrine block is a building forming the abbot's house, with two rooms on each storey and a SE wing, also with two rooms on each level.

The abbey was only suppressed in 1563 and monks still periodically used parts of the abbey throughout the 17th century. The last monk is said to have lived until 1752.

MUNSTER ABBEYS & FRIARIES 55

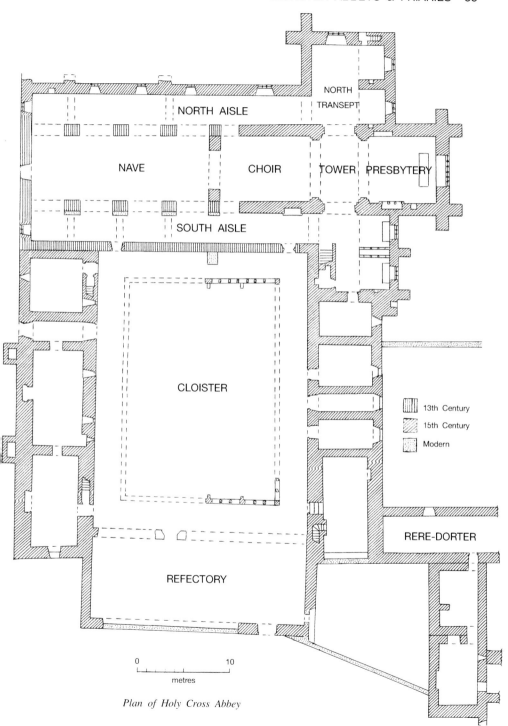

Plan of Holy Cross Abbey

Looking across the former cloister garth of Hore Abbey

HORE ABBEY Co Tipperary   S070408   0.8km NW of Cashel

In 1272 David MacCarwill, Archbishop of Cashel had some Cistercian monks from Mellifont sent to take over a monastic site originally occupied by Benedictine monks from Glastonbury brought over by Philip de Worcester in the 1190s. The community was initially well endowed and was able to build a complete new set of buildings by c1300, although it later declined. Only low walls remain of the cloister and its garth and of the west and north ranges, but more survives of the east range, with a sacristy next to the church, a latrine block or reredorter at the north end, and a chapter-house projecting to the east, with a small later window replacing its original triple east lancets.

The church on the south side has a standard Cistercian layout with an aisled nave of five bays, transepts each with two eastern chapels and a short presbytery with triple east lancets and sedilia and a piscina on the south side. In the 15th century the north and south arches of the crossing were closed up and a rib-vault inserted under the tower, whilst the southern chapels (which had been enlarged at some point) were abandoned and walled off. A new wall was built between the second and third bays of the nave and several of the arcade arches on each side were blocked up. See p58.

INCHICRONAN PRIORY Co Clare   R391856   10km NE of Ennis

In 1189 Donal Mor O'Brien had Augustinian canons sent over from Clare Abbey to take over a monastery founded by St Cronan. The church has a good east window of c1200 and a south doorway. It had become parochial by 1302 despite its very remote location at the end of a 1.5km long peninsular which almost divides the lough in two. A north sacristy and a south transept with a two bay arcade were added in the 15th century along with a domestic range extending south from the west end of the nave.

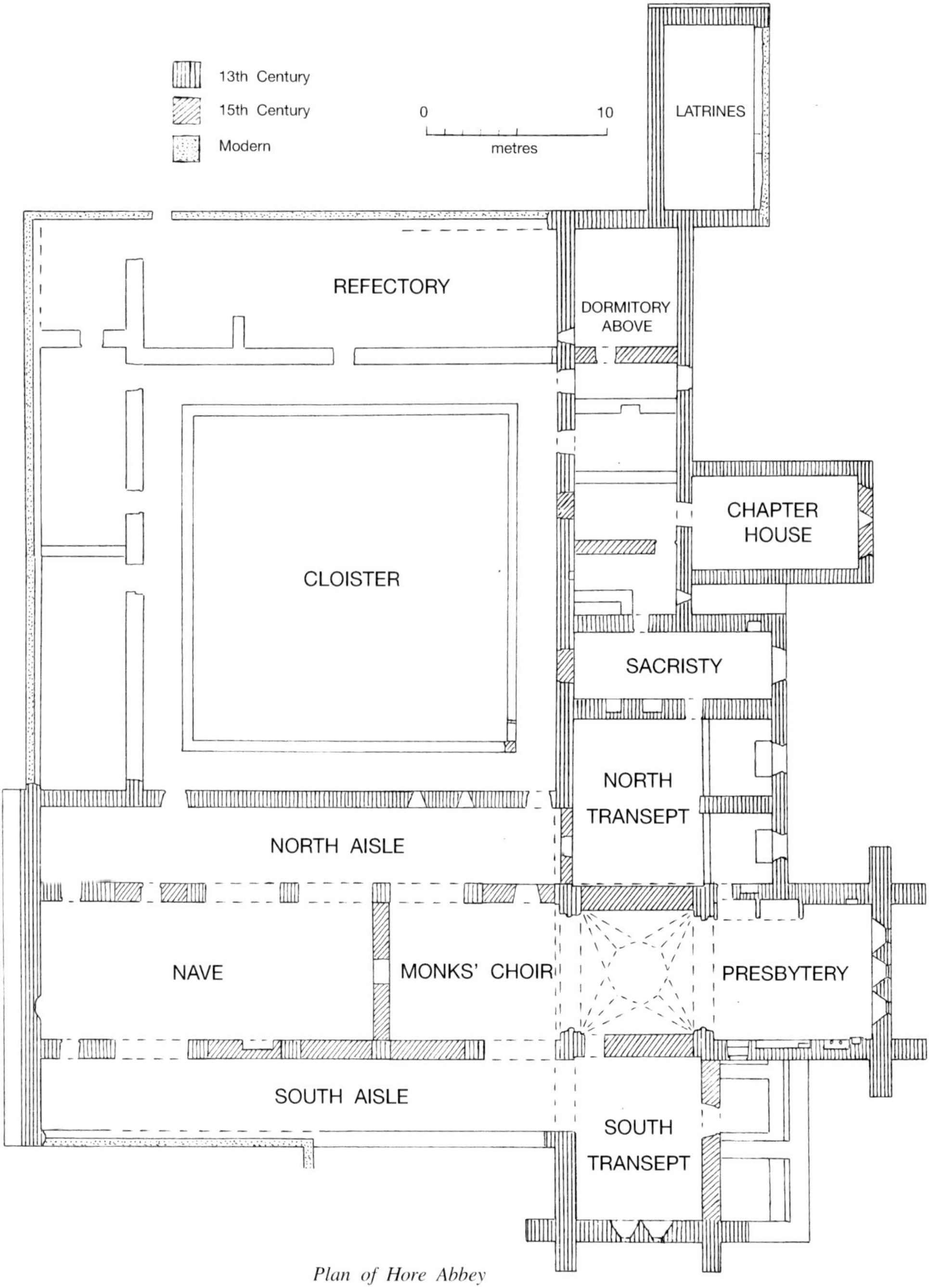

MUNSTER ABBEYS & FRIARIES 57

- ▥ 13th Century
- ▨ 15th Century
- ▦ Modern

0 — 10 metres

LATRINES

REFECTORY

DORMITORY ABOVE

CHAPTER HOUSE

CLOISTER

SACRISTY

NORTH TRANSEPT

NORTH AISLE

NAVE | MONKS' CHOIR | PRESBYTERY

SOUTH AISLE

SOUTH TRANSEPT

Plan of Hore Abbey

Hore Abbey

INISHLOUNAGHT ABBEY   Co Tipperary   S176214   4km WSW of Clonmel

A Protestant church incorporates a window, a Transitional style door-head of three orders and tomb fragments from a Cistercian abbey founded in the 1140s by Melaghlin O'Phelan of the Deise for monks from Monasteranenagh. The door-head is a relic of major building works in progress in the 1190s with Donal Mor O'Brien as patron.

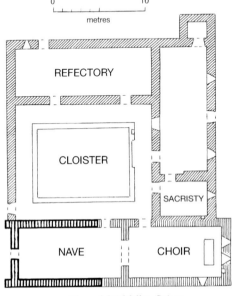
Plan of Inishfallen Priory

INNISFALLEN PRIORY Co Kerry V935894 Island in Lough Leane

This monastery founded by St Finian in the 7th century was noted for its learning. One monk, Maelsuthain O'Carroll, d1009, was said to be the best doctor in the western world. Here c1215 were written the Annals of Inisfallen, an important source of early Irish history. Later in the 13th century the main early church with antae was extended eastwards with a new chancel. In 1320 the community adopted the Benedictine rule. A small cloister was added on the north side with an east range containing a dormitory over three rooms and a north range containing a refectory. A 12th century oratory with a fine west Romanesque doorway lies above the shore 18m away.

The abbot's niche at Kilcooly

Kilcooly Abbey

KILCOOLY ABBEY Co Tipperary   S291580   5.5km ESE of Urlingford

In 1182 Donal Mor O'Brien founded this abbey of St Mary and St Bernard for Cistercian monks from Jerpoint. The church was built c1210 but was wrecked by warfare in 1445 and lost its aisles when it was rebuilt by Abbot Philip O'Brophy, d1463, whose tomb lies in the presbytery. Other monuments include a tomb chest of c1526 with figures on side-panels and an effigy of Piers Fitz Oge Butler of Clonamicklon with the signature of its sculptor Rory O'Tunney. Of the same period are monuments to William Cantwell and Margaret Butler and John Cantwell and Elicia Stoc, whilst those of James Stoc and Margaret Butler and Richard Cantwell and his wife Grace are of c1590-1610.

The presbytery has a vault carried on inserted piers and heavy corner buttresses and a six-light east window with reticulated tracery. Other 15th century parts are the transepts, with another vault over the northern one, and the rectangular central tower, two of the piers of which are hollowed out as splendid seats for the abbot and prior. The wall between the south transept and the sacristy has carvings of the Crucifixion, St Christopher, an ecclesiastic, and a mermaid with a mirror and a fish. Part of the east range around the cloister survives. The massive hall-house to the SE was probably an infirmary. By the approach to the abbey is a circular vaulted dovecot.

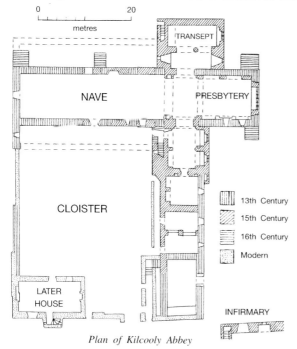
Plan of Kilcooly Abbey

Kilcrea Friary

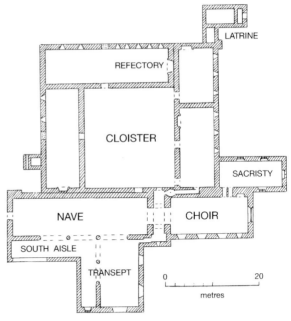
Plan of Kilcrea Friary

KILCREA FRIARY   Co Cork   W510682   16km WSW of Cork

Cormac MacCarthy, Lord of Muskerry founded this friary for Observant Franciscans in 1465. Its buildings, which are unusually complete, appear to be entirely of the following thirty years or so. The church has a central tower, a choir, a south transept with a two bay arcade towards a western aisle and a nave with a three bay arcade towards a south aisle, both arcades having circular piers. The choir has remains of a four-light east window with intersecting tracery and four south windows and a piscina. On the north side is a tomb recess and a gap marking where there was a doorway to a sacristy, over which was a well-lighted scriptorium. The transept has a large south window and two each windows each flanked by a piscina for a former altar. The transept aisle south end has a hood-moulded window with two ogival-headed lights. The nave has remains of a large west window over a doorway.

Corbels for the roofs are the only traces of the cloister alleys. Evenly spaced windows suggest that there were dormitories divided into small cubicles on the upper floors of the west, north and east ranges, the latter having a stair leading down into the space under the tower. The crosswall and the two fireplaces in the lower storey of the east range are later insertions. At the NE corner is a latrine block. The north range lower storey seems to have had a passageway between doorways roughly in the middle. East of it the range contained a refectory with five tall single-light windows facing north. The area west of the passage is now filled by a 19th century mausoleum. The west range also seems to have had a cross-passage on the lower level. Both storeys here have fireplaces in the south gable and there is a latrine block adjoining the west wall. The friary was suppressed in 1542 but in practice the friars stayed on under MacCarthy patronage until the 1650s. The friary was sacked in 1584 and again a few years later, but was repaired in 1603 and in the 1620s.

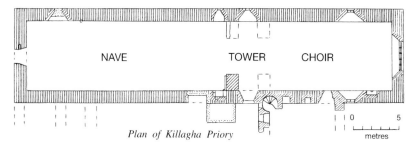

Plan of Killagha Priory

KILLAGHA PRIORY   Co Kerry   Q820011   1km NW of Milltown

Geoffrey de Marisco installed Augustinian canons here c1220, replacing an older monastery founded by St Colman. In the early 14th century the priory was important enough for its prior to have a seat in Parliament. Only slight traces remain of a cloister about 18m square on the south side, the buildings around it having been destroyed by Cromwellian troops c1650. The church measuring 40m long by 7.2m wide internally is mostly 13th century but the west doorway is the only certain feature of that date. The five-light east window, windows with pairs of narrow lights on either side of the choir, and the double piscina date from a remodelling in the 15th century. Only one pier remains of a narrow central tower then inserted. The northern room of the east range was a sacristy entered from the church. It retains a spiral staircase in the NW corner.

KILLONE ABBEY   Co Clare   R323733   4.5km SSW of Ennis

This Augustinian nunnery is first mentioned in 1260 but it is assumed to have been founded by Donal Mor O'Brien in the 1190s. The two round-headed east windows with lozenges on the rere-arches and a passage with trefoiled heads through their embrasures are probably of c1225-40. Below this end is a vaulted crypt. The narrower west end of the church was divided off in the 15th century, when much of the north wall was rebuilt and three ranges were built around a small cloister to the south. The east range is more complete than the others and has a reredorter set at the SE corner.

Nunnery ruins at Killone   *Kilcrea Friary*

62   MUNSTER ABBEYS AND FRIARIES

Tomb recess at Kilmallock Friary   *Pier adorned with ballflowers at Kilmallock Friary*

KILMALLOCK FRIARY Co Limerick   R609280   To E of Main St, near N end

Gilbert, second son of John, Lord Offaly is said to have founded this Dominican friary in 1291. Of that period must be the five graduated east lancets separated only by slender mullions with banded inner shafts and an inner hoodmould with head-stops, and also the row of six two-light windows with Y-tracery facing south. Work on the church was continued under patronage of Gilbert's son Maurice, the first of the series of White Knights. There is a broken tomb of the last of the White Knights, Edmund FitzGibbon, d1608, who betrayed the "Sugan" Earl of Desmond to the English. The 14th century south transept has a western aisle with a two-bay arcade with a circular pier adorned with ball-flowers, common in English churches c1310-45 but very rare in Ireland. The huge end window of the transept with reticulated tracery, however, is thought to be a 15th century insertion, as is the central tower. The transept and the original domestic buildings (later much altered and extended) were probably complete by 1340, when a General Chapter of the order was held here.

In 1594 the friary was leased to Nicholas Miagh but was soon reclaimed by the Crown for non-payment of the rent. At some point the friars returned, for two of them were executed by the Cromwellians in 1648.

Kilshanny Priory   *Dominican Friary at Limerick*

KILSHANNY PRIORY   Co Clare   R136926   5km N of Ennistimon

A church of c1200 with a Transitional style north doorway and south window remains of a small Augustinian priory founded by Donal Mor O'Brien on the site of a monastery of St Seannach. The west doorway, the easternmost southern window and the east window with intersecting tracery over sub arches are late medieval.

KINSALE FRIARY   Co Cork   W635506   To NW of town centre, outside the walls

Minor featureless fragments remain of a Carmelite friary founded in 1334 by Robert FitzRichard Balrain. It was reported in 1541 as having a church with a belfry, cloister, hall and other buildings and was much damaged during the siege of Kinsale in 1601. A temporary chapel built in 1633 was abandoned in 1653, but there were still friars here as late as 1741, when the prior was appointed as the town almoner.

LIMERICK FRIARY   Co Limerick   R579579   To NE of Limerick Castle

Only the long north wall of the church with several 13th century windows, including one with Y-tracery, remains of a Dominican friary founded in 1227 by King Donnchadh Cairbreach O'Brien, who was buried here in 1241. Some of the former domestic buildings to the north were probably sponsored by James, 6th Earl of Desmond, buried here in 1462. Pope Innocent X raised the friary to the status of a university in 1644 for the Catholic Confederation of Kilkenny.

LISLAUGHTIN FRIARY   Co Kerry   R004461   6.5km WSW of Tarbert

John O'Connor Kerry founded this friary for Observant Franciscans in 1478 and by 1507 the buildings were complete enough for a Chapter of the order to be convened here. The church is 36m long and has an east window with intersecting tracery with a central oval, south windows of two ogival-headed lights under label hood-moulds, and sedilia, whilst the short south transept has an end window of four stepped lancets set within a square frame. Ogival-headed tomb-recesses with side pinnacles lie on the north side of the nave. The slender central tower has collapsed some time since the 1780s. The north and west ranges around the cloister to the north are very ruinous but the east range still lies complete with an upper dormitory with space for twenty cubicles and a latrine block at the north end. To the NW is the precinct gateway. After being suppressed the friary was granted to the Herbert family, but some friars remained, three of them being strangled in front of the high altar by English troops in 1580. They formally gained possession again in 1629 and probably remained until the 1650s.

Lislaughtin Friary

64   MUNSTER ABBEYS AND FRIARIES

Lorrha Augustinian Priory

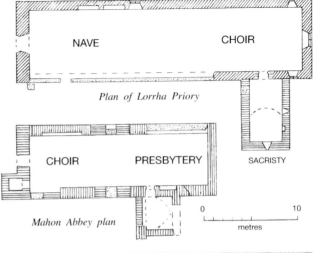

Plan of Lorrha Priory

Mahon Abbey plan

Lorrha Dominican Friary

LORRHA FRIARY   Co Tipperary   M916045   6km E of Portumna

The church of the Dominican friary founded in 1269 by Walter de Burgo, Earl of Ulster is 44m long by 7.7m wide internally and has a double piscina and a row of six paired late 13th century lancets on the south side. A block of masonry to the west of them is all that remains of a 15th century central tower. The nave has remains of single lancets and a three-light later medieval south window. The west end with its doorway, window and bellcote has been rebuilt by the Office of Public Works since collapsing in 1939.

LORRHA PRIORY   Co Tipperary   M919046   6.5km E of Portumna

The 15th century church of this Augustinian priory has a west doorway with an ogival hoodmould with crocket finials. In the head of the doorway is a woman's head adorned with a horned headdress and collared robe once painted in blue and gold. The window above has two trefoil-headed lights with a quatrefoil over and a hood-mould with a label-stop. Other windows are single and twinned ogival-headed lights, but not much remains of the east window and most of the south wall is missing. There is an added two storey sacristy on the south side. A prior of Lorrha is mentioned as late as 1599, but in 1643 Augustinian friars took over the buildings abandoned by the canons.

MUNSTER ABBEYS & FRIARIES 65

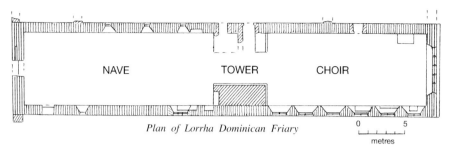

Plan of Lorrha Dominican Friary

MAHON ABBEY Co Cork   W491429   10.5km ENE of Clonakilty

The Cistercians from Aghmanister moved to this location in the 1270s (see page 77). By 1541 the church had a long-established use for parochial worship and the core of it was adapted for Protestant use. It is now an ivy-clad oblong 21m long by 8m wide with traces of blocked arches to transepts. The east wall of the south transept and a vaulted chapel still remain. The west end is late medieval and has two-light windows over a doorway and a tall but thin tower on the SW corner. At the SW corner of the former cloister to the south stands a four storey late medieval tower, also clad in ivy.

MOLANA ABBEY Co Waterford   X080828   6km NW of Youghal

The 7.5m wide nave of a church on an island in the Blackwater estuary incorporates walling from an early church of a monastery founded by St Molana in the 6th century. It became Augustinian in the 12th century and survived until 1541. The choir added in the 13th century has long rows of lancets on each side and remains of a large east window in which a smaller window was set in the later medieval period, when a sacristy with an upper storey was added on the north side. A cloister court 15m wide extends 20m southwards from the nave. Four doorways lead into the east range, where three lancets show where the chapter-house lay. The refectory in the south range is ruinous but preserves a window which lighted the reader's pulpit. The west range contained a kitchen with a well. A wall extending south from the east range contains a gateway.

West doorway detail at Lorrha Priory

South side of the choir at Molana Priory

66 MUNSTER ABBEYS AND FRIARIES

Monasteranenagh Abbey

Monasternagalliaghduff

Plan of Monasteranenagh Abbey

■ 12th Cent
□ c1200-10
▥ 13th Cent
▨ 15th Cent

MONASTERANENAGH Co Limerick R549409 3.5km E of Croom

Turlough O'Brien, King of Limerick founded this abbey c1150 for Cistercian monks from Mellifont. It was one of the largest Irish abbeys and the abbot was a lord of Parliament. The church was 55m long with an aisled nave and a short presbytery with triple east lancets wrecked by the collapse of the vault in 1874. The transepts each with three east chapels were walled off in the 15th century and little remains of them, a 17th century mausoleum having replaced the one chapel on the south. The blocking walls under the north and south crossing arches of c1180-90 has helped to preserve the finely carved foliage capitals on the engaged shafts. A tower above fell in 1807. Also 15th century are the thick wall at the west end of the monks' choir and the blocking walls of the four bays of arcades of c1190-1210 with pointed arches on square piers. Further west there are solid walls between the nave and aisles. Two round-headed lancets remain in the nave west wall. In 1365 there was a nearby battle in which Brian O'Brien and the MacNamaras defeated the King of Thomond, who took refuge in the abbey but was captured and ransomed. The abbey was officially suppressed in 1541 but the monks remained until 1579 when an English force under Sir Nicholas Malby defeated Sir John of Desmond nearby and then bombarded the abbey, where the Irish took shelter. All the monks were killed and most of the domestic buildings around a cloister measuring 32m by 30m on the south side were wrecked. Minor fragments and footings remain of the west and south ranges and rather more of the chapter-house projecting from the east range, where triple east lancets survive.

MUNSTER ABBEYS & FRIARIES   67

MONASTERNAGALLIAGHDUFF PRIORY   Co Limerick R280472 nr Shanagolden

Hidden behind a farmhouse, disguised by trees and vegetation, are remains of the 13th century Augustinian nunnery of St Catherine de O'Connell, first mentioned in 1298. Walls enclose all four sides of a cloister court about 25m square. The refectory on the south side has remains of a reader's pulpit. Another range extends south from its west end. Parts of a west range also survive, with fireplaces in a crosswall. The church 27m long by 6m wide internally extends from the middle of the east side of the cloister. Its fine shafted entrance without a door rebate is like that of a chapter-house, which would normally be located on this side of a cloister. A piscina and one sedile remain on the south side but ivy obscures what remains of the eastern and other windows.

MOOR FRIARY   Co Tipperary   R811279   1km E of Galbally

This Franciscan friary was founded in 1471 probably by the O'Briens of Aherlow. The building destroyed by fire in 1472 may only have been a temporary structure rather than the existing church ruin, which has a lofty central tower. The friary formed a strongpoint during Queen Elizabeth's reign and was burned by English troops in 1569. Despite this there were still friars here the following year when three of them were mutilated and killed by the English forces. Even in the early 20th century the friary was a focus for anti-English forces, causing the Royal Irish Constabulary to attempt to blow it up.

MOTHEL ABBEY   Co Waterford   X397164   5km S of Carrick-on-Suir

St Brogan founded a monastery here in the 6th century. It adopted the Augustinian rule in the 12th century and survived until 1540, when there was a church and steeple, five chambers, a dormitory and a kitchen, the church probably being parochial. There are remains of the south wall of the church with parts of three windows, the west gable with a doorway that possibly led to a vanished west tower, and footings of a south chapel. Nearby lie side panels from the tomb of Abbot Rory O'Comoyn, c1500.

MOURNE ABBEY   Co Cork   W571933   6.5km SSE of Mallow

Of the preceptory of Knights Hospitallers founded c1200 no domestic buildings remain but there are ivy-clad walls of a church with a chancel 14m long (now lacking most of its east end) added later to a nave 29m long by 8.2m wide internally. The church lies on the north side of a walled enclosure near the confluence of the Abbey and Clyda rivers. The court is gable-shaped and about 70m wide and extends 90m from the SE side to the small D-shaped NW tower. About 40m south of this tower is a more substantial rectangular tower, perhaps the "strong fortified tower" which John Fitz-Richard was required to build after being appointed prior in 1335. The west end of the tower has gone and not much of it still stands above a fragmentary vault with a mural chamber in the south haunch. A 7m length of the curtain wall north of the tower is 3m thick.

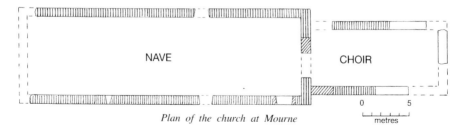

Plan of the church at Mourne

Muckross Friary from the SW

MUCKROSS FRIARY   Co Kerry   V974870   4km S of Killarney

Founded by Donal MacCarthy in 1448 for Observant Franciscans and mostly complete by 1475, this is one of best preserved friaries in Ireland, with a delightful location near Lough Leane. It has a church 33m long by 7m wide with a central tower and an added south transept of c1500 with niches for two east altars and an end window with intersecting tracery. The choir east window of four lights also has intersecting tracery. The south windows are of two or three lights with ogival heads and there is one window with an unusual stepped head under the tower, which has a rib-vault. A sacristy on the north side of the choir extends east of the eastern range of the buildings set around a cloister 14m square on the north side. The cloister is complete with vaulted alleys with arcades of five arches on the east and north and six on the west and south. These support the upper walls of the ranges, where the rooms are spacious and well-lighted in contrast to the vaulted stores below which are lighted only by narrow loops. A latrine at the NE corner served the dormitory in the east range, whilst the north range contains a refectory with a reader's pulpit. A later wall containing fireplaces divides it from a kitchen in the west end of the range. The west range used by the guardian contains the entrance passage and also a north facing door beside a staircase. The only other entrance to the complex is the finely moulded nave west doorway.

The friary was suppressed in 1641 and leased in 1587 to the Earl of Clancarty. By 1602 the friars had returned and were restoring the buildings. They were driven out in 1629 but returned and remained here until driven out by the Cromwellians in 1652.

NENAGH FRIARY   Co Tipperary   R866791   In SE part of town

Much of the late 13th century church 43m long by 7.8m wide internally still remains of a Franciscan friary founded by Donogh O'Kennedy a year or two before he died in 1252. It became the chief Franciscan house in Ireland, hosting a provincial synod of the order in 1344. The church has three huge east lancets taking up almost the whole end wall, and the north side has a row of ten sandstone lancets with conjoined embrasures, and five single lancets further west, some of them altered or blocked up. The west doorway and the bellcote above it are 15th century. Part of a sacristy remains at the SE corner. The cloister and its buildings on this side seem to have been destroyed in Elizabeth I's reign but Observant Franciscans used the friary from the 1630s until the 1650s.

MUNSTER ABBEYS & FRIARIES 69

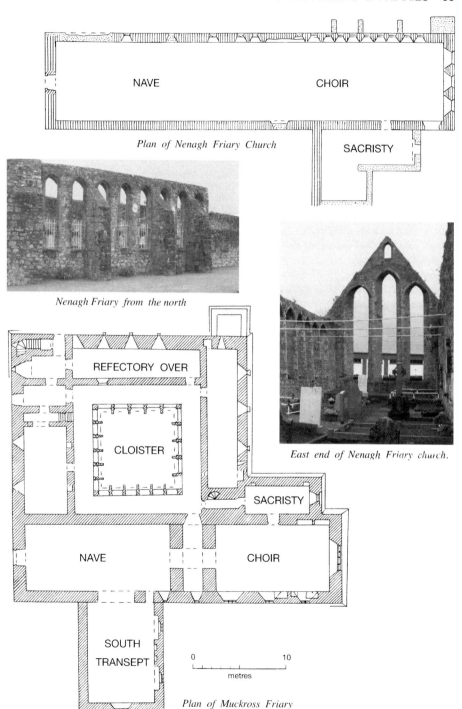

Plan of Nenagh Friary Church

Nenagh Friary from the north

East end of Nenagh Friary church.

Plan of Muckross Friary

QUIN FRIARY   Co Clare   R419745   On east side of River Rine at Quin.

Grafted onto the remaining lower parts of Thomas de Clare's small courtyard castle of 1280 with three surviving circular corner towers is a well-preserved friary established for Observant Fanciscans by Maccon MacNamara in 1433. The church incorporates parts of the 3m thick castle walls and the south windows have two or three lights set in the middle of the wall with deep splays both inside and out whilst the east window of three lights with intersecting tracery with trefoiled sub-arches opens off a recess deep enough to accommodate the high altar. There is a sacristy on the north side and a slim 27m high embattled central tower with a rib-vault over the lowest stage. The south transept added c1500 has set-back corner buttresses, a three light end window and a pair of two-light windows for altars with a piscina adjoining each one. There is a tomb in the choir NE corner and the nave has a tomb recess on the north side.

The cloister court 16m wide has arcades of six bays on the north and south sides and of seven on the east and west sides. These arcades support the inner walls of the three upper rooms, which all seem to have been dormitories lighted by simple single rectangular openings, one for each friar's cubicle. At the NE corner a small reredorter or latrine block is connected by an arch to the main building. The lower storey of the north range contained a refectory served by a long narrow kitchen with two fireplaces in the west range. The central doorway in the west range is modern. The only original entrances to the complex were doorways in the nave west wall and onto a passage at the north end of the east range. One stair rises from this passage and another lies at the east range south end. One window in the west range has two tall cusped ogival-headed lights with decorated spandrels under a hoodmould with leaf stops. Both the church and the ranges have wall-walks with remains of outer parapets.

Quin Friary

MUNSTER ABBEYS & FRIARIES 71

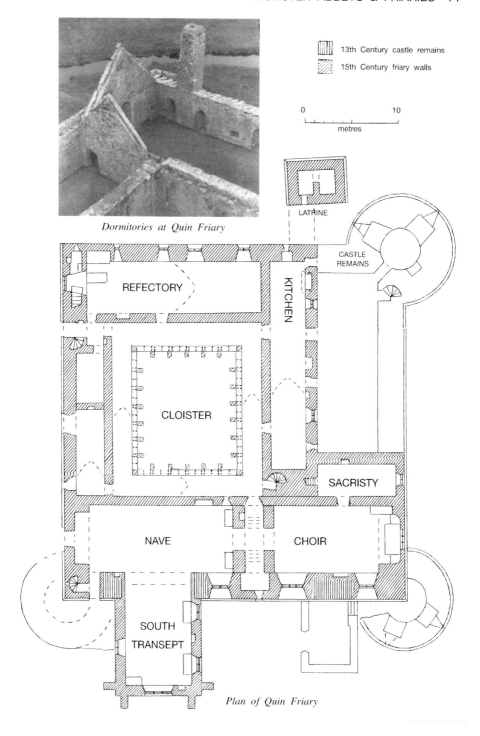

Dormitories at Quin Friary

Plan of Quin Friary

RATHKEALE PRIORY Co Limerick R367417 Towards E end of Rathkeale

Most of the 13th century church of the Augustinian priory of St Mary founded by Gilbert Harvey still stands. The row of south lancets are original but the four-light east window with intersecting tracery is probably later medieval.

RATTOO PRIORY Co Kerry Q880336 7.5km SSE of Ballybunnion

A fine east window of three lights with flowing tracery over sub-arches remains in the 15th century church of an Augustinian hospital. The south wall contains a doorway and two damaged windows once of two lights and three single-light windows.

RINCREW PRECEPTORY Co Waterford X095809 3.5km NNW of Youghal

A 13th century church 18m long by 8m wide on a ridge above a bend of the Blackwater formed part of a preceptory of the Knights Templar. The eastern parts of the north and south walls remain, each with traces of two large windows. A vaulted sacristy on the north side partly blocks one window. The larger two storey building further west on the north side is later. The raised platform measuring 20m by 17m on the south may represent a former cloister.

ROSCREA FRIARY Co Tipperary S135891 On south side of Roscrea

Remains of a Franciscan friary founded in the mid 15th century comprise the crenellated central tower, the north walls of the nave and choir, and the east wall of the latter with its window blocked by an adjacent house. In the north wall are two windows of two ogival-headed lights with sunk spandrels under hoodmoulds. A road runs along the north side so the cloister must have been unusually located on the south side. A dormitory, hall, prior's chamber, chapel garden and two orchards are mentioned in 1568. Material from the site was taken c1800-10 to build an adjacent church.

Rathkeale Friary   *Roscrea Friary*

MUNSTER ABBEYS & FRIARIES 73

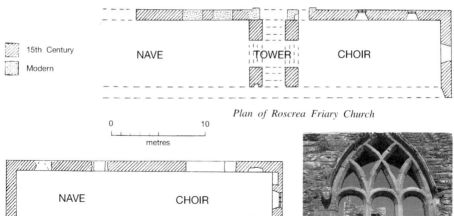

Plan of Roscrea Friary Church

Plan of Rattoo Priory Church

Sherkin Friary

ROSS PRIORY   Co Cork
W286364   On S side of Ross Carbery

The Benedictine priory founded c1218 was already in ruins by 1541. Of it there remain the ruinous north and south walls of an oblong church 18.5m by 7.5m with corbels for a possible cloister on the south and a doorway on the north side.

SHERKIN or FARRANACOUSH FRIARY   Co Cork   W027257   E side Skerkin Isd

Fineen O'Driscoll established Observant Franciscan friars here in 1449, although their church was probably not begun until the 1460s. It has a nave and chancel divided by a fairly low (15m) central tower and an arcade of three arches on square piers leading into a south transept with paired lancet windows and two east chapels. The nave and choir each have end windows with sub-arches under intersecting tracery. There is a vine-leaf terminal to the south end of the eastern arch under the tower. To the north is a cloister with remains of three ranges. The east range has vaulted lower rooms. Vaults in the west range have collapsed and the south wall of the north range has gone. Additions probably of after the friary was burned in 1537 by the men of Waterford are the gabled building between the west and north ranges and the three storey sacristy block between the east range and the choir. After suppression the friary was held by a series of tenants and in the early 17th century was purchased by Sir Walter Coppinger. About that time the friars returned to live in a house purchased for them in 1627.

THURLES FRIARY   Co Tipperary   S128586   On east side of river at Thurles

The Catholic Cathedral of the Assumption lies on site of a Carmelite friary founded c1300. It was already ruined by c1540, when it had a church, chapter-house, three chambers and a stable. Old descriptions suggest the church had a tower and a north transept. In 1557 the site was granted to the Earl of Ormond. The friars seem to have returned periodically and still had some establishment in the area in the 1730s.

TIMOLEAGUE FRIARY   Co Cork   W472436   9km ENE of Clonakilty

The choir of this friary for Observant Franciscans set on the west bank of the mouth of the Argideen River has unusually thick walls with a passage going through the embrasure of the triple lancet east window and side windows originally of paired lancets set in tall and deep recesses. There are wall-walks with the parapets projected on widely spaced and roughly made corbels. The windows suggest a date of c1280-1300 but they are probably just old-fashioned work of the early 14th century under MacCarthy patronage. However there is a possibility the friary was actually founded by the de Barrys at an earlier period and the eastern half of the nave (which is lower than the choir) could actually be mid to late 13th century in origin. The south transept with a west aisle with a three bay arcade and a projecting east chapel is clearly a later addition, perhaps of the 15th century, and some rebuilding of the original three bay arcade of the south aisle of the nave was required to accommodate it. The end window with three triple stepped lancets again looks like work of c1300, but it could possibly have been reset from the original nave west wall or is simply 15th century work in the old style.

   The lower fourth and fifth arches of the south arcade may be 15th century, which is the period of the east range of the well preserved buildings around the cloister. Next to the choir is a sacristy and projecting to the east is a latrine block. There are cellars below. The westernmost bay of the nave was probably added along with the narrow central tower by Edmund Courcy between 1494, when he was created Bishop of Ross Carbury, and 1518, when he was buried in the friary here. He also added the western range containing a kitchen, the north range with a library set over store-rooms, the refectory extending at an awkward angle from the NE corner and the infirmary beyond it with an eastern latrine projection. The windows are all plain except for two on the east side of the refectory, one of them rebuilt by the Board of Works along with parts of the cloister arcading of the same period. Beyond the west range is an outer court.

   In 1577 the friary was granted to James Barry, Viscount Buttevant, who leased it to tenants. It was ransacked by an English force during the wars of the 1580s and all the stained glass windows smashed. However repairs were carried out in 1604 and there were still friars based here in 1629 when Brother Michael O'Cleary came down from Donegal to copy manuscripts from the Book of Lismore kept in their custody.

Timoleague Friary

MUNSTER ABBEYS & FRIARIES 75

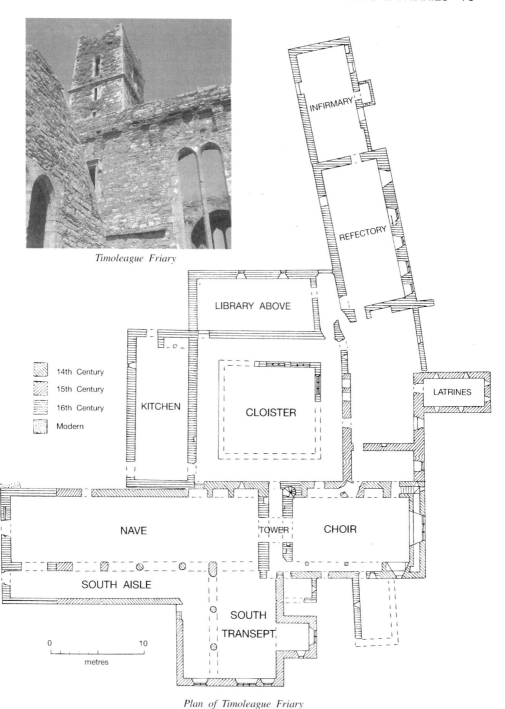

Timoleague Friary

Plan of Timoleague Friary

TOOMEVARA PRIORY Co Tipperary R977775 In village, 11km E of Nenagh

This Augustinian priory of St Mary was founded in the mid 12th century on the site of an older monastery of St Donain. In 1541 Donogh O'Meara, a descendant of the original patron, was adding a tower to the priory buildings which may have remained ruinous since 1450, when the warden reported that the convent was too poor to repair its war-damaged buildings. The buildings were still ruinous and the tower incomplete when granted in 1597 to Miler MacGrath. The church seems to have been parochial in later years and has been much rebuilt. Two 15th century features of interest are the tomb chest with an effigy now outside and the south doorway with traces of what appears to be an internal porch projecting into the church. A cloister may have lain to the north and there are remains of another building to the north, perhaps a church.

TYONE PRIORY Co Tipperary R876782 1.5km SE of Nenagh

In c1200 Theobald Walter founded this priory and hospital of St John the Baptist which was served by Augustinian Crutched friars. It was made secular under a warden in 1541 but was suppressed ten years later. The 13th century church was much altered and rebuilt in the late 15th century but some of the later single and two-light windows were set into older embrasures. Only the bases of the northern piers now remain of the central tower inserted in the 15th century. A range running south from the nave has remains of a series of vaulted chambers and a spiral staircase. Another fragment lies to the east and part of another building lies SW of the church.

WATERFORD FRIARY Co Waterford X607124 In centre of walled town

Remains of the Dominican friary of St Saviour established by 1230 comprise the north wall of the choir, a four storey central tower and the nave 17m long by 5m wide internally with five lancets facing north and three blocked pointed arches on the south to a former aisle. In 1541, when it was suppressed and leased to James White, the friary also had a dormitory, chapter-house, library, kitchen, three halls, a store and other rooms. It was granted to Sir Anthony St Leger in 1599 and was used as a courthouse during the 17th and 18th centuries.

WATERFORD FRIARY Co Waterford X610124

Known as "The French Church" through being used for worship by French Hugenot refugees in the late 18th century, this was a Franciscan friary established by 1245. The church has a rib-vaulted and embattled five storey central tower set between a choir with triple east lancets and three windows in the south wall and a nave with blocked lancets on the north side and a blocked three bay arcade on the south. Only the east end remains of the aisle, with a four light east window and one of three lights facing south. North of the choir is a sacristy. The outward facing upper doorway in the nave west wall was inserted after the nave became a hospital of the Holy Ghost in 1545. When suppressed five years previously the friary had a hall, kitchen and bakehouse, six chambers, four cellars and two stables.

Dominican Friary at Waterford

WATERFORD PRIORY   Co Waterford   X610121   In Catherine St
During the 1580s, when a Spanish invasion was expected, Edmund York supervised the erection of an earthwork fort around the buildings of the former Augustinian priory of St Catherine possibly founded by Prince John during his brother's reign in the 1190s. A star-shaped fort around four roofed ranges is shown on a map of 1590 and the ruins are shown on late 17th century maps. A courthouse now occupies the site.

YOUGHAL FRIARY   Co Cork   X010785   To N, outside of walled town
The late 13th century west gable of the church with a three-light window and a few other low fragments remain of a Dominican friary of the Holy Cross founded in 1268 by Thomas Fitz-Maurice FitzGerald. In 1289 and 1304 it was the scene of General Chapters of the Dominican Order. Sir Walter Raleigh dismantled parts of the friary after obtaining a grant of the buildings in 1586. He sold it to Richard Boyle in 1602.

Only loose fragments remain of a Franciscan friary at the south end of the town (X107776) founded in 1224 by Maurice FitzGerald. Little remained of it by the 1680s. After the suppression the friars moved to a house at Curraheen in Co Waterford.

YOUGHAL PRIORY   Co Cork   X104782   On SW side of Main Street of Youghal
A much altered gable with a late-medieval sandstone doorway, pointed under a square hood-mould, is a relic of a Benedictine priory of St John first mentioned in 1306.

OTHER MEDIEVAL MONASTIC SITES IN MUNSTER
ABBEYFEALE Co Limerick   R114265   Cistercian Abbey founded by Brian O'Brien in 1188 lay by river. It was annexed to Monasternenagh in 1204.
AGHMANISTER Co Cork W464417 Footings of church & cloister of Cistercian abbey founded in 1172 by Dermot MacCormac MacCarthy. Moved to Mahon c1270 (p65)
BANTRY Co Cork V982442   Loose fragments from Franciscan friary suppressed in 1542 in graveyard. Wrecked by English in 1568. Levelled by O'Sullivan Bear 1602.
CASTLECOR Co Cork R449069 Two low fragments may be relics of a former priory, probably of Augustinian canons, mentioned in a late 13th century document.
CHORE Co Cork W881735   C of I church on site of small Cistercian abbey or cell.
CULLEN Co Cork W232904 Possible site of rather doubtful former nunnery.
GLANAWYDAN Co Waterford X436011 Traces of parish church on site of Cistercian daughter-house of Inishlounaght suppressed as early as 1228 because of decline.
KILMONEY Co Cork W720622 Gable of church of cell of Augustinian Gill Abbey at Cork. Probably reduced to merely a vicarage by the mid 14th century.
KILBARRY Co Waterford X595103 Small fragment of small church of preceptory of Knights Templars, later Hospitallers, later parochial, and still in repair in 1615.
KNOCKAVERY Co Cork X108770 Site of small nunnery of St Anne founded c1190, gone by 1644. The nuns tended a beacon light on a small adjacent round tower.
LEGAN Co Cork W765661 Site of small Benedictine priory church.
MOLOUGH Co Tipperary S137142 Remains of church and traces of domestic ranges of nunnery of St Brigid. An early foundation revived in 14th century by the Butlers.
TRACTON Co Cork W731565 1819 C of I church on site of Cistercian abbey of 1225 founded by Odo de Barry with monks from Whitland. Loose frags at Abbey House.

LEINSTER ABBEYS AND FRIARIES

ABBEYDERG PRIORY   Co Longford   N141164   9.5km S of Longford

The east end of the church with triple east lancets and two single ones facing south remains of an Augustinian priory founded c1205 by Gormgall O'Quin of Rathcline.

ABBEYSHRULE   Co Longford   N227589   7km NE of Ballymahon

The O'Farrells of Annaly had Cistercian monks sent over from Mellifont c1200 to found this abbey on the east bank of the Inny. It was rebuilt after being burned in 1476. The remains of the aisleless 40m long church are very overgrown and the surviving Transitional style details are hard to see. Between the nave and chancel there is a vaulted passage flanked by other vaulted spaces. This deep screen rises up to support a double bellcote. At the SE corner of the former cloister stands an equally overgrown tower with a round tower turret which may date from after Sir Robert Dillon, Chief Justice of the Court of Common Pleas obtained the site from Queen Elizabeth in 1569.

AGHABOE FRIARY   Co Laois   S327858   8.5km NE of Rathdowney

This Dominican friary founded by Florence MacGillapatrick in 1382 was suppressed in 1540. The church retains a three-light east window and the remains of four south windows each of two lights, west of which is a south transept added c1500 with a three light south window and a pair of two-light east windows, below which were altars. Unusually there is a doorway near the end of the south wall of the nave as well as one in the west end wall. Very little remains of the north wall, beyond which was a cloister.

    The semi-octagonal bell-turret of an Augustinian priory of 1234 replacing an older monastery founded by St Canice in the 6th century stands at the NW corner of the 19th century Protestant church. There are carved heads beside the turret doorway and on the side of the church which is said to have windows taken from the friary.

AGMACART PRIORY   Co Laois   S331745   6.5km SE of Rathdowney

The original monastery dating from 550 was burnt in 1156 and by 1168 the MacGillaprick Lord of Ossory had had it replaced by an Augustinian priory of which just the NE corner of one building now stands. Other fragments lie beside the Protestant church to the SSW. Grose shows the church as having a tower, and there was a gateway to

Baltinglass Abbey

Arches into transept at Aghaboe

BALLYBOGGAN PRIORY Co Meath N636403 4km S of Clonard

The 13th century church of the Augustinian priory founded by Jordan de Cumin is impressive for its size of 58m by 8m but it has lost most of its transepts and hardly any cut stone remains of its features, which included paired lancets on each side of the choir and a 15th century tomb recess on the north side. Only humps and bumps remain of the cloister and its buildings on the south side. The priory was very wealthy and when suppressed held 5,000 acres of good arable and pasture land in Meath.

BALTINGLASS ABBEY Co Wicklow S868889 At N end of Baltinglass

The east end of the 56m long church of this Cistercian abbey founded in 1148 was later used for Protestant worship and has a tower of 1815 to the west of the original crossing, over which an oblong tower was raised in the 15th century. The round south arch of the crossing remains, together with the east end with three lancets and sedilia. Of an aisled nave of c1200 there remains the west front with a triplet of now headless lancets over a doorway and an arcade of eight plain pointed arches between the nave and south aisle. Two piers are round, with scalloped capitals, but the rest are square. The two eastern chapels of each transept were each separate projections, which is not a normal Cistercian layout. A late medieval tower with a SE corner turret which formed the abbot's house was demolished to provide materials for a rectory built in 1882.

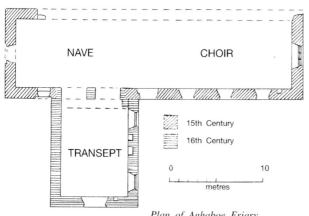

Plan of Aghaboe Friary

Aghaboe Priory

Ballyboggan Priory

BECTIVE ABBEY   Co Meath   N860599   6.5km NE of Trim

In January 1147 Bective became the first daughter house of the Cistercian abbey at Mellifont, itself then only five years old, land being donated by the King of Meath, Murchadh O'Melaghin. The church was once 47m long with a six bay aisled nave and transepts each with two chapels. In the 15th century the domestic buildings and cloister were entirely rebuilt on a smaller scale since the number of monks had dropped. At that time the church lost its aisles and the last bay of the nave, gaining a new west front with two corner turrets and a new central tower, under which the arches to the transepts were reduced in width. The only older parts, all of c1275-1300, are the south arcade of the nave with its series of blocked pointed arches and a clerestory of quatrefoil windows above, parts of both transepts and the square chapter house with two east windows and a vault with a central pier. The western and southern ranges have upper rooms extended over the cloister alleys with arcades formed of triplets of cinque-foiled pointed arches set on dumb-bell shaped piers. One of these piers is carved with a figure holding a crozier. Adjoining the ranges to the west is a tower with a SW corner stair turret which probably formed the abbot's house.

The claustral buildings have survived better than the church because after the abbey was suppressed in 1537 (when it held 4,400 acres of land in Meath) Thomas Agard adapted them as a residence, adding a third storey with a four-light end window over the dormitory in the east range. The refectory served as his great hall with new south windows, the sacristy by the south transept became a bakehouse and chimneys were added then or a few years later to the south and east ranges. Agard was succeeded by other powerful occupants, Lord Chancellor John Allen from 1544, then from 1552 Treasurer Andrew Wyse, who in 1559 was succeeded by Sir Bartholomew Dillon. From 1639 the former abbey was held by Richard Bolton, Chief Baron of the Exchequer.

CALLAN FRIARY   Co Kilkenny   S416440   N side of river, E of main road

This church is thought to have been built c1470 by James MacRisderd Butler to serve an Observant Augustinian friary established a few years earlier by his father Eamon. The church has a low central tower, a good west doorway and end windows and a very ornate triple set of sedilia with ogival heads with crocketed finials and pinnacles set under a master canopy. Nothing remains of the sacristy and the domestic buildings.

Callan Friary

LEINSTER ABBEYS AND FRIARIES 81

Bective Abbey

Cloister at Bective Abbey

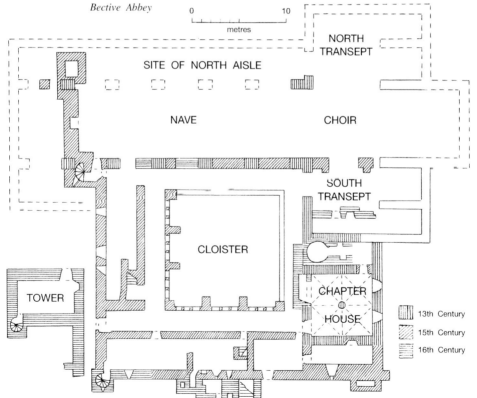

Plan of Bective Abbey

82 LEINSTER ABBEYS AND FRIARIES

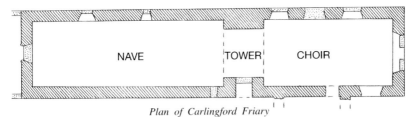

Plan of Carlingford Friary

CARLINGFORD FRIARY Co Louth J190114 In village of Carlingford

A church 39m long by 7m wide internally still survives of a Dominican friary probably founded c1305 by Richard de Burgh. It has a central tower set over unusually wide arches, with a stair-turret at the SE corner. Just ragged holes, most of them blocked up, remain of five large windows in the choir. The nave has a blocked west doorway, two north windows and traces of a cloister roof on the south. In the 15th century the west end wall was remodelled with a parapet with a machicolation and two corner turrets. Just the south end remains of a 14th century range extending south from the choir. A 15th century tower-like building adjoins it on the east at the south end.

CASTLEDERMOT FRIARY Co Kildare S782848 At S end of Castledermot

The Franciscan friary plundered by Edward Bruce in 1317 and suppressed in 1541 is first mentioned in 1247 as the recipient of royal alms. It was enlarged in 1302 by Thomas, Lord Ossory when the choir was lengthened and a north transept added with both a western aisle and a set of three eastern chapels with three-light windows with intersecting tracery, possibly its earliest appearance in Ireland. One these chapels must have been the Lady Chapel in which Thomas, 2nd Earl of Kildare, another major benefactor, was buried in 1328. The transept end window was destroyed c1810. In the 15th century a tower was added on the north side of the choir. The nave retains two lancets over a central doorway in the west wall and others facing north. A row of skeletons was revealed by the collapse of part of the south wall. The domestic building further south is probably 15th century. Part of a precinct wall retains on the north side.

A plain 15th century tower at the north end of the town is the only relic of a friary for Augustinian "crutched" friars founded c1220 by Walter de Riddlesford.

Castledermot Friary

LEINSTER ABBEYS AND FRIARIES

CLONMACNOISE NUNNERY Co Offaly 015309   12km SSW of Athlone

This is the burial place of Dervorguilla, wife of Tiernan O'Rourke of Breffny, whose abduction by Dermot MacMurrough of Leinster led to Dermot's expulsion and the eventual Anglo-Norman invasion. She retired here in 1170, having sponsored the building of a nave and chancel church and the introduction of Arroasian canonesses (although there were nuns here as early as 1026). The church has a partly renewed chancel arch of three orders with chevrons, heads and interlacing and a west doorway of four orders with animal heads on the capitals. There are footings of a domestic building to the NW of the church and traces have been noted of other buildings further east. There is no certain evidence that the cathedral complex was ever served by Augustinian canons.

CLONMINES FRIARY Co Wexford S844129   1km SW of Wellingtonbridge

Most of this 28m long by 7.5m wide church for Augustinian friars existed by the late 14th century, having been founded by the Kavanaghs c1317 and further patronised by Nicholas FitzNicholas in 1385. A three bay arcade opens into a narrow aisle with two small windows. The choir has remains of a large east window, three large south windows and a piscina and triple sedilia. A turret was later added to the west end of the aisle and a central tower inserted in the eastern half of the nave. A spiral stair against the NW pier of the tower blocks an earlier three-light window. The staircase served a room over the vault and also allowed access to wall-walks on both nave and choir.

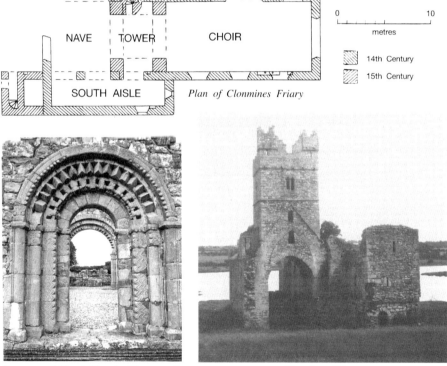

Doorway of Nuns' Church, Clonmacnoise   *Clonmines Friary*

DROGHEDA FRIARY   Co Louth   O089755   To N of town centre

All that remains of a Dominican friary founded c1224 by Luke Netterville, Archbishop of Armagh is the slender central tower (known as Magdalene Tower) with fine transomed belfry windows of two lights inserted into the 13th century church in the early 15th century. Drogheda also had a Franciscan friary founded c1245 located at 090756, and a friary for Augustinian Crutched friars at 088743.

DROGHEDA ABBEY   Co Louth   O086752   To W of town centre

The Augustinian abbey and hospital of St Mary d'Urso founded by Ursus de Swemele c1206-14 stood outside the west gate of the walled town. The 15th century central tower with a vault and transomed two-light belfry windows and the 13th century choir still remain, the latter preserving only a south doorway and the outline of a large later east window. Modern walls outline the former nave, which had a north aisle of which the west gable still survives. Just a hint of the shape and size of the cloister on the south is given by fragments of its western and southern bounding walls.

DUBLIN ABBEY   Co Dublin   O155345   Off Mary's Abbey Street, N of R. Liffey

This abbey of St Mary was originally founded in 1139 for Savigniac monks and became Cistercian in 1147 when the two orders merged. It rapidly outgrew its adopted mother house of Buildwas in Shropshire and became the largest and most wealthy monastery in Ireland. During the 15th century Government records were stored at the abbey and meetings of the Privy Council were held within it. When suppressed in 1539 the abbey had an annual income of over £537. In England only Fountains and Furness could top that amongst Cistercian abbeys. Lord Leonard Grey took over the spacious abbot's lodgings as his own mansion, but in 1541 he was executed on a charge of treason.

All that remains standing is the chapter-house of c1200 with triple east lancets and a rib-vault in four bays, plus a vaulted slype or passage on its south side. These parts seem to have survived the fire of 1304 which necessitated considerable rebuilding elsewhere. The original church was large, probably had three chapels to each transept, and was covered with a lead roof paid for by Felix O'Ruadan, Archbishop of Tuam, who was buried here in 1238. In the chapter house has been set up a single bay of a cloister of c1440 discovered in Cook St in 1975, then assumed to have been part of the abbey, although it now seems more likely to have come from Christchurch cathedral priory.

DUBLIN CATHEDRAL PRIORY   Co Dublin   O152335   SSW of city centre

The crossing, transepts and probably the east part of the crypt of Christchurch Cathedral are of the 1180s, although the north transept was rebuilt in the 1870s, when a new east end replaced a long late medieval choir and a fine doorway was moved from the north transept to the south transept. In the nave 13th century work of both beauty and importance survives in the upper parts of the north arcade, but piers are of the 1870s, along with most of the south side, west front and all the aisle windows.

In 1163 Archbishop Laurence O'Toole installed Augustinian regular canons to serve the cathedral, which had been founded by a Norse King of Dublin c1030. Very little has survived of the cloister on the south side and the buildings around it apart from the lower parts of a chapter-house of the 1220s with a fine doorway. The High St now covers the site of the refectory. The fragment of a cloister arcade of the 1440s now in the Cistercian abbey chapter house probably came from here. The cathedral is more fully described and illustrated in the companion volume: Medieval Churches of Ireland.

LEINSTER ABBEYS AND FRIARIES 85

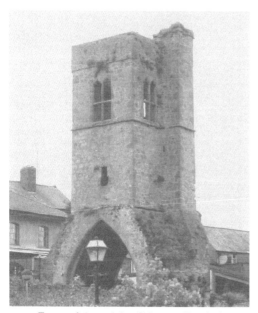

Tower of Augustinian Priory at Drogheda

Tower of Dominican Friary at Drogheda

Romanesque doorway at Christchurch, Dublin

Chapter house doorway at Christchurch, Dublin

Duiske Abbey, Graiguenamanagh

DUISKE ABBEY Co Kilkenny   S710438   On E side of Graiguenamanagh

Also known as Graiguenamanagh, this has one of the largest of the Irish Cistercian abbey churches. It was founded in 1207 by William Marshal for a party of monks from Stanley in Wiltshire, and has a 60m long church with an aisled nave of seven bays and transepts each originally with three east chapels. More complete than most Irish monastic churches, and now roofed again for Catholic worship, it has nevertheless lost the end chapel of each transept, plus the rib-vaulting which rose from filleted shafts in three bays over the presbytery and also the central tower (which is said to have had an octagonal top) which collapsed in 1774, taking with it the eastern parts of the nave arcades, which have been replaced by solid walls. The presbytery has large original early 13th century lancets, some of them round-headed. The transepts have cusped circular windows over the chapels. The south aisle retains a very fine round-headed doorway with complex mouldings including tiny chevrons and the inner arch multi-cusped.

A cloister garth 36m square lies to the south but its buildings are rather neglected and partly hidden amongst later structures. Only one long fragment remains of the west range but considerable parts remain of a kitchen and refectory on the south side. In a later remodelling a new refectory was extended out to the south with a reader's pulpit in its west wall. The east range has a sacristy next to the south transept, then a treasury followed by the original chapter house with a triple west opening. East of this a large new chapter house was later added. To the SE are the east walls of a series of rooms which either formed the infirmary or the abbot's house.

In 1346 the abbot was fined for harbouring outlaws. After suppression in 1541 the abbey went to the Butlers and was sold to the Agars in 1703. The two high crosses in the graveyard east of the buildings have been brought in from elsewhere.

LEINSTER ABBEYS AND FRIARIES

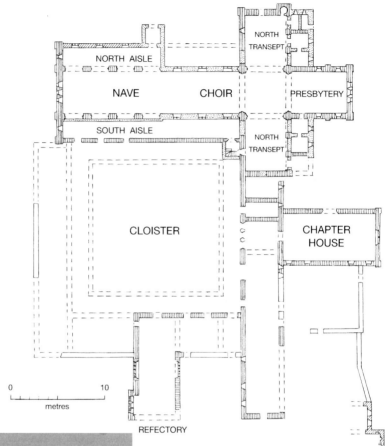

Plan of Duiske Abbey

The presbytery at Duiske Abbey

The much-altered east range at Duiske Abbey

88 LEINSTER ABBEYS AND FRIARIES

DULEEK PRIORY   Co Meath   O046684   In village 8km SW of Drogheda

There was an early monastery here founded in 488 by St Ciaran. The imprint of its vanished round tower remains on the north side of a 15th century tower at the west end of the church of Mary which seems to have part of an Augustinian priory founded in the 1180s by Hugh de Lacy. The tower has a stair turret at the SW corner and large belfry openings with transoms. Of the nave only the south wall with four arches towards a 14th century aisle now remains. There is a tomb chest of a 15th century member of the Plunkett family, an effigy of a late 17th century bishop of Meath, and the east window of 1597 has below it the arms of Sir James Bellow and Dame Ismay Nugent.

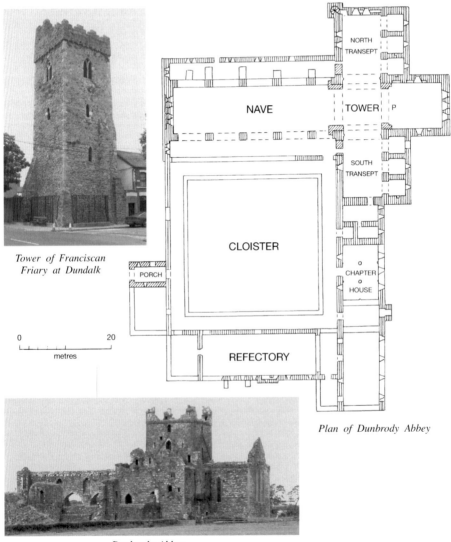

Tower of Franciscan Friary at Dundalk

Plan of Dunbrody Abbey

Dunbrody Abbey

DUNBRODY ABBEY   Co Wexford   S710151   1.5km W of Campile Station

Hervey de Montmorency founded this Cistercian abbey in the 1170s, making it a condition that the abbey should offer a sanctuary for all malefactors, and later becoming its abbot. His nephew Herlewin, Bishop of Leighlin supervised its construction and was buried here in 1216. The abbey was involved in various disputes in the 1340s, firstly refusing to be inspected by the then presumed mother house at Dublin (Buildwas in Shropshire had been the original mother house) resulting in the deposition of the abbot. It was then seized by Edward III's officials because the monks gave no hospitality or alms. In 1355 the abbot and two monks were accused of stealing horses from monks of neighbouring Tintern abbey but were acquitted. The abbey was made independent about that time and in the 1370s the abbot was mitred and recognised as a lord of Parliament. The abbey was suppressed in 1537, the last abbot becoming Bishop of Ferns, and in 1546 the abbey was granted to Sir Orborne Etchingham, who made it into a mansion, inserting many square-headed windows. His descendants the Chichesters handed it over to the Office of Public Works in 1911.

Most of the 58m long church still remains, although the south arcade collapsed in 1852 and the aisle wall on that side is reduced to foundations. Each transept has three groin-vaulted east chapels and there is a night stair in the south transept. The east end of c1200-10 has three tall and wide stepped lancets. A tower 11m square was later raised over the crossing, the original round arches then being obscured by inserted pointed ones. The surviving arcade of c1240-50 has five pointed 13th century arches with soffit-ribs which are set on square piers with chamfered corners, above which are positioned the clerestory windows of one or two trefoil-headed lights. Parts of the cloister 36m square remain with a refectory with a reader's pulpit on the south and just a porch surviving on the west. The east range has a sacristy next to the church, and a treasury between it and the chapter house with its triple arched entrance, south of which is a passage. Not much remains of the dormitory above these rooms.

Dunbrody Abbey

DUNDALK FRIARY   Co Louth   J053075   To NE of centre of Dundalk

The late 14th century four storey Seatown Tower with wicker-centring marks on the vault is a remnant of a Franciscan friary which is first mentioned in 1246. The parapet and NW top turret appear to be later but the Y-traceried belfry windows are original.

DUNDALK FRIARY   Co Louth   J051075   To NE of centre of Dundalk

The only relic of St Leonard's, a house of Augustinian Crutched friars founded by the Verdun family in the 1180s or 90s is a vaulted room in the county library grounds.

90 LEINSTER ABBEYS AND FRIARIES

FERNS PRIORY   Co Wexford
T023497   To NW of cathedral in Ferns

Of the small Romanesque church of an Augustinian priory founded in 1160 by Dermot MacMurrough there remain the north walls of the nave and the narrower chancel which was vaulted. A doorway from the nave leads to a vaulted sacristy with a stair to an upper room. Set against the northern part of the nave west wall is a tower which is square below but round higher up. The 13th century building with rows of lancets on either side but the end walls missing which is located east of and in line with the cathedral may have been intended as a new choir for this priory. See page 92.

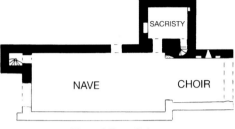

Plan of Ferns Priory

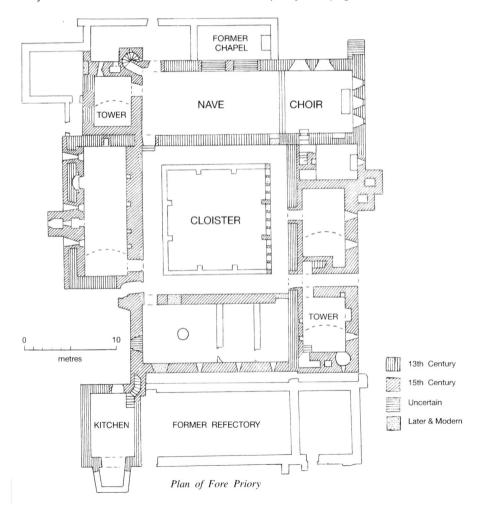

Plan of Fore Priory

FORE PRIORY Co Westmeath   N511708   At Fore, 5km E of Castlepollard

In the 1180s Hugh de Lacy established a Benedictine priory dedicated to St Taurin and St Fechin here as a dependency of the abbey of St Taurin at Evreux in Normandy. It was never poor and had a yearly income of £100 when suppressed, but numbers declined in later years. In 1340 there were just a prior and six monks, and by the early 15th century the tiny community was in a difficult position, open to attack by the Irish on the one hand and technically an alien priory on the other. In 1449 Parliament proclaimed it an independent priory. About that time, when William England and William Croys (appointed 1441) were successively priors, and the priory formed the NW outpost of the Pale, it was largely rebuilt with a smaller and more defensible new layout.

The triple east lancets of the choir are the only certainly earlier feature, although the south wall of the church, the kitchen now left projecting at the SW corner and the west walls of each of the east and west ranges do contain 13th century masonry. East of the kitchen are footings of the original 13th century refectory superseded by a new one further north in the 15th century rebuilding. This later refectory and the west range appear to lie within the space of the original larger cloister. Both the east and west ranges contain vaulted lower rooms, those in the west range having double-splayed loops, and the upper rooms have fireplaces, window-seats and latrines in small projecting turrets. There is a tower built over the vaulted sacristy south of the church and another with a NE stair turret lighted by crossloops was inserted into the west end of the church. The east arcade of the cloister has been re-erected using fragments excavated in 1912. It has cinquefoiled pointed arches. Two arches blocked up in 1870 in the nave north wall originally opened into a side-chapel.

Cloister at Fore Priory

Fore Priory

92 LEINSTER ABBEYS AND FRIARIES

The priory church at Ferns

St Saviour's Priory at Glendalough

Plan of St Saviour's at Glendalough

GALLEN PRIORY Co Offaly 118236 1km SSE of Ferbane

About 200 graveslabs dating from the 8th to the 11th century remain from an early monastery founded c492 by St Canoc. Excavations have revealed footings of a small 11th century church altered in the 13th century. The community adopted Augustinan rule in the 12th century and later built a new church further south. Featureless since the 15th century east window with Flamboyant tracery collapsed a few years ago, although carved fragments lie amongst the rubble, it measures 22m by 6m internally and has a transept projecting 7.5m from near the east end of the north wall.

GLASCARRIG PRIORY Co Wexford T215493 By coast 11km SSE of Gorey

Just one 13m length of featureless walling remains of a priory of St Mary for monks of the Order of Tiron established in 1193 as a daughter of St Dogmaels Abbey in Pembrokeshire. A hall, two rooms and a chantry and yard still accompanied the church in 1560, seventeen years after it was suppressed.

GLENDALOUGH PRIORY Co Wicklow T133966 1km W of Laragh

Although founded in 1162 for Arroasion canons, this church of St Saviour has fine but restored features more likely to be of c1200 in its two-light east window and chancel arch. The chancel was once vaulted and the nave has two windows on the south side. The doorways at either end of the nave south wall suggest a possible small cloister there but the only domestic building standing is a large extension of uncertain date adjoining the north side. It has a staircase in its east wall. For descriptions of the other churches at Glendalough see the companion volume Medieval Churches or Ireland.

GRACE DIEU PRIORY   Co Dublin   O181525   4km SW of Lusk

A few gravestones and traces of the cloister are all that remain of an Augustinian nunnery. Most of the buildings were dismantled in 1565 by the Barnwalls to provide material for building Turvey House. The nuns had retired to Portraine after a petition by the local gentry stating the convent's good reputation and usefulness to the English colony within the Pale had (inevitably) failed to save it from being suppressed.

GREAT CONNELL PRIORY   Co Kildare   N817141   2km SE of Newbridge

There are only minor remains of this Augustinian priory founded in 1202 by Myler FitzHenry, as a daughter-house of Llanthony in Monmouthshire. The chief item of interest is an effigy of Prior Walter Wellesly, d1539, who was also Bishop of Kildare and Master of the Rolls. Carved panels from the tomb chest are set in the graveyard wall. A second ecclesiastical effigy remains beside the nearby Protestant church. In its heyday this was a very important monastery and its prior had a seat in Parliament.

INCHMORE PRIORY   Co Longford   N284860   On island 9km NW of Granard

This was an early monastery on an island in Lough Gowna which later adopted the Augustinian rule. There are remains of a church with three windows of c1180-1200.

INISTIOGE PRIORY   Co Kilkenny   S634379   In middle of Inistioge, W of river

A 19th century Protestant church lies on the site of the choir and makes use of the central tower of an Augustinian priory of St Mary and St Columba founded c1206-10 by Thomas FitzAnthony, Seneshal of Leinster. There also still remains a second tower further north which has an octagonal upper stage over a square base. Probably of c1400, it now forms a mausoleum containing an effigy of Mary Tighe, d1810. In her day the Lady Chapel still survived in use as the parish church.

The two towers of the priory at Inistioge

JERPOINT ABBEY   Co Kilkenny   S572402   2km SW of Thomastown

The church here may have been begun for Benedictine monks under patronage from 1158 by Donal MacGillapatrick, King of Ossory, but in 1180 Cistercian monks from Baltinglass arrived to take over and the resulting building is typically Cistercian. It had an aisled nave with arcades of six bays, transepts each with two vaulted eastern chapels and a short presbytery covered by a barrel-vault, over which was an attic in the roof. On the north side at this end are tomb-recesses, one with an effigy of Felix O'Dulany, Bishop of Ossory from 1178 to 1202. There are also effigies of two late 13th century knights and of Robert Walsh, d1501 and Katherine Poer. On the south side is a piscina and three sedilia which are round-arched with a spiky edge roll-moulding.

The nave has three round-headed lancets in the west wall. The surviving north arcade of c1180-1200 has plain pointed arches with hood-moulds carried on very short piers with scalloped capitals which are set on the remains of screen walls. The western piers are square with angle-shafts but two round piers occur further east where the monks' choir was situated. Above the piers are round-arched single-light windows in deeply splayed embrasures. The crossing arches were altered in the 15th century when an embattled tower with corner turrets was added, along with a large new east window with fine tracery. At that time the cloister was extended northwards to occupy the space of the former south aisle. It was provided with new arcades of round arches set on dumb-bell shaped piers with carvings of figures, animals and floral motifs on the sides, parts of which have been re-erected. Nothing remains of the lay brothers' rooms in the west range and only fragments remain of the refectory on the south side set north-south between a kitchen and a warming room. The east range is fairly complete work of c1200 with a sacristy next to the transept and then a chapter house.

Jerpoint Abbey

Cloister at Jerpoint Abbey

LEINSTER ABBEYS AND FRIARIES 95

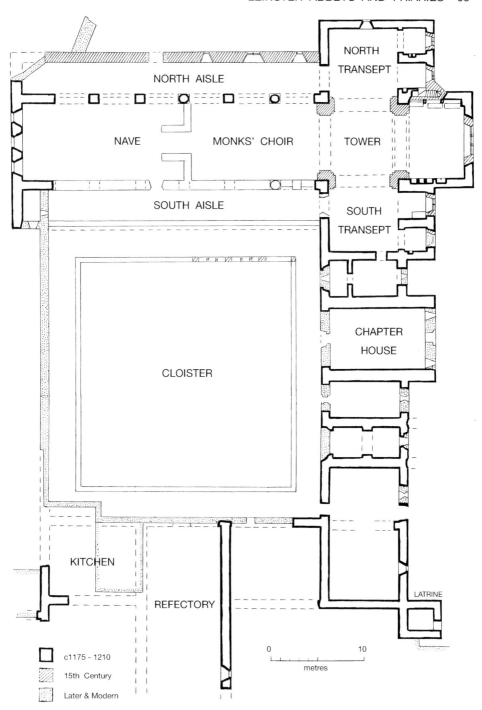

96 LEINSTER ABBEYS AND FRIARIES

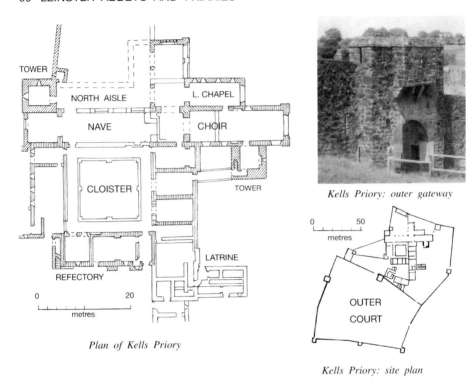

Kells Priory: outer gateway

Plan of Kells Priory

Kells Priory: site plan

KELLS PRIORY Co Kilkenny   S498432   13km S of Kilkenny

This Augustinian priory of St Mary was founded c1193 by Geoffrey FitzRobert de Montemarisco, seneshal of Leinster. The priory was suppressed in 1540 and granted to the Earl of Ormond but the community survived in some form or other and continued to elect priors until the 1640s. The 54m long church had a central tower with a short south transept and a long north transept with a western aisle. The choir is flanked by a Lady Chapel on the north and a second tower probably serving as a sacristy on the south. A passage connected the tower's SW doorway (beside a staircase) to the east range. The nave had a north aisle and there was a third tower at the NW corner. The few surviving details suggest most of it is now late medieval, which is certainly the period of the two extra towers, which are both about 8m square externally. There is also a west range. The 18m square cloister and its buildings to the south are fragmentary. On the east side was a chapter house and there was a latrine block projecting from the dormitory SE corner, whilst on the south side was an upper storey refectory which still has twinned lancets. The buildings lie in an inner precinct backed onto a stream on the north side and having a crenellated wall on the south with a gateway next to a tower, with another gate by a tower on the east. South of here another court about 100m wide extends 80m up the slope. It has a remarkably complete wall about 1m thick rising 4m to a coving (there is no wall-walk). Towers containing upper storey living rooms with fireplaces and latrines for officials or guests lie at the southern corners and along the south and west sides, whilst the east side has a gateway covered by a machicolation. This is the best preserved monastic precinct in Ireland, covering five acres.

The church at Kells Priory

KILCULLEN FRIARY Co Kildare N847092 By R. Liffey, 1km ESE of Kilcullen

The only relics of this friary for Observant Franciscans founded in 1486 are fragments of the tomb of its founder Sir Roland FitzEustace of Harristown, d1496, and his wife Margaret Jennico, which in Penal times were set in the wall of a mass-house. Another FitzEustace effigy from here lies in the Protestant church at Ballymore Eustace.

Kells Priory fom the south, showing wall of inner precinct

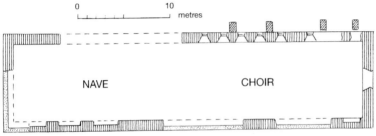
Plan of Kildare Friary

KILDARE FRIARY Co Kildare   N728120   0.5km SSW of Kildare

The church of the Franciscan friary founded in the 13th century by the de Vescis is now very fragmentary, although a row of five lancets and an extra single one remain in the north wall of the choir, which has later buttresses. The tomb recesses on the south side of the nave may be associated with the FitzGerald earls of Kildare, eight of whom were buried here. There is no trace of the Lady Chapel added by Thomas, 2nd Earl , d1328. Possibly it was a north transept. There was also once a Carmelite friary at Kildare.

KILKENNY FRIARY Co Kilkenny   S504560   NW side of city, S of cathedral

Within the yard of Smithwicks' brewery lie the choir and central tower of the church of a Franciscan friary founded by Richard Marshal in 1232. The choir was extended in 1321 with a splendid east window of seven stepped lancets and a set of three trefoil-headed sedilia separated by slender columns. The tower was under construction in 1347, making it one of the earliest of its type with a square belfry set over a vaulted crossing area with piers and wide arches across the church. The belfry is lighted by windows with pairs of ogival headed lights with a transom. During this period friar John Clyn was writing his noted annals here.

Kildare Friary

St John's Priory at Kilkenny

Franciscan Friary at Kilkenny   *Dominican Friary at Kilkenny*

KILKENNY FRIARY   Co Kilkenny   S505561   Towards N end of city centre

The 13th century nave and the 14th century south transept of the Dominican friary of the Holy Trinity founded by the younger William Marshal in 1225 were re-roofed in 1788-93 and re-opened as a Catholic parish church in 1840. Inside are a 15th century alabaster carving of the Holy Trinity, a 16th century Flemish image of the Virgin Mary and a crude oak figure of St Dominic dating from Penal times. The large transept with its western aisle and huge five-light end window with complex tracery with intersections adorned with pointed and unpointed quatrefoils had probably only just been completed by 1349, when the Black Death ravaged the population of the city and eight of the friars died in a single day. The embattled square central tower with corner turrets and some of the windows are insertions of the 15th century. The friary was suppressed in 1541 and then used as a courthouse, but it was briefly restored as a church in the 1640s when the Confederate Catholics were in control of Kilkenny. Nothing has survived of the choir demolished c1780 or of the cloister and its buildings.

KILKENNY PRIORY   Co Kilkenny   S509561   Between city centre and station

Much of the Augustinian priory and hospital of St John founded c1220 by William Marshal the younger was removed in 1780 to make way for a barracks but the Lady Chapel of c1300 on the south side was renovated for use as a Protestant parish church in 1817, when it was given a west tower. It was once known as the Lantern of Ireland because windows in the form of stepped trefoil-headed lancets filled almost all the wall-space. The roofless choir adjoining it has seven east lancets and a tomb-chest of c1500 of a couple of the Purcell family. There are also minor remains of the nave and other buildings. During the Confederate Catholic occupation of the city in the 1640s the titular prior allowed the Jesuits to set up a training college in the priory.

The Dominican Friary at Kilkenny

KILLEIGH PRIORY Co Offaly N365182 SW of village, 8km SSE Tullamore

In the 12th century an Augustinian priory replaced an older monastery said to have been founded by St Sincheall in the 5th century. In the 14th century Murrough O'Conor introduced Franciscan friars, who seem to have taken over the older buildings. Part of the priory church, now lacking the central tower and SW transept shown in a sketch of 1896, is used as a Protestant church. The east end has been shortened and the original triplet of lancets lies nearby in the graveyard wall. Within the farmyard of the late 16th or early 17th century house to the north lies the chapter house with traces of an east window and wall-shafts of the early 13th century, although the vault and part of the north wall are later medieval. A staircase in the NW corner leads to an upper room with gunloops inserted later and there is a possible latrine on the NE corner.

KILTEEL PRECEPTORY Co Kildare N983212 SW of Kilteel, 10km E of Naas

A 15th century tower with an adjoining gateway remains of a preceptory of the Knights Hospitaller founded c1250 by Maurice FitzGerald, 2nd Lord Offaly. It was suppressed in 1541, after which it was granted to Sir John Allen. Four Chapters of the Order were held here between 1326 and 1334, shortly after which Robert Clifford was ordered to repair the defences. There are vaults over two of the five storeys on the tower.

LARAGH ABBEY Co Longford N366797 At Abberlara, 4km SE of Granard

In 1214 this Cistercian abbey was established by monks from St Mary's at Dublin on lands given by Richard Tuite before he was killed three years earlier. In 1318 the northern Irish chiefs complained to Pope John XXII that the monks hunted the local Irish during the day and sang vespers in the evenings. The abbey subsequently declined and several buildings had gone or fallen into ruin before it was suppressed in 1540. All that remains is the much altered central tower of the church, a later addition set over the 13th century crossing arches, one of which remains complete on the west side. A blocked arch is visible on the south side, where there is a weathered carving variously interpreted as a Virgin and Child or a varient on a sheila-na-gig.

LEINSTER ABBEYS AND FRIARIES 101

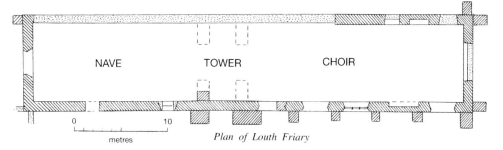

Plan of Louth Friary

LOUTH PRIORY Co Louth H956014   To NW of Louth, 11km SW of Dundalk

A 14th century church 47m long by 7.8m wide internally remains of an Augustinian priory founded in 1148 which replaced the monastery founded by St Mochta in the 6th century. The large east window and the five south windows mostly now lack tracery but one window had intersecting tracery and the one in the nave has a rere-arch carried on corbels with dog-tooth on one capital and an animal head on the other. Most of the north side has been replaced by a modern wall but there is evidence of a former sacristy of two storeys towards the east end. There are only slight traces of a central tower inserted in the late medieval period, when buttresses were added along the south side. Near the top of the third buttress from the east is a 12th century fragment with a pellet motif. Two similar fragments are reset into the west pier of the graveyard gateway. Part of a round tower to the south remained until at least 1835.

Gateway and tower at Kilkeel Preceptory

The lavabo at Mellifont

102 LEINSTER ABBEYS AND FRIARIES

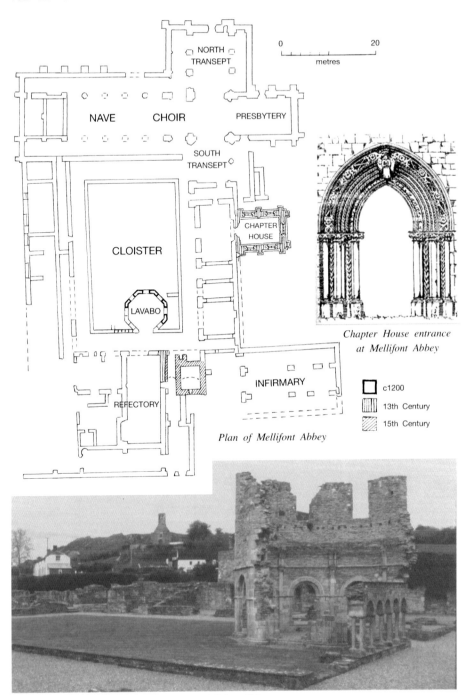

Chapter House entrance at Mellifont Abbey

Plan of Mellifont Abbey

Mellifont Abbey

MELLIFONT ABBEY   Co Louth   O012780   8km NW of Drogheda

In 1142 St Malachy of Armagh brought over Cistercian monks from Clairvaux in France to found the first house of that order in Ireland. By 1170 there were 100 monks and 300 lay brothers here, and colonies had been sent off to no less the six daughter-houses. The French monks had returned home after falling out with the Irish monks who were disinclined to observe strictly all the statutes of the order. By the 1220s both Mellifont and its daughter houses were accused of being lax and suffering insubordination and it took several years to sort out their problems, the abbot of Mellifont eventually being forced to resign. The abbey was plundered by local nobles in 1494. After the abbey was suppressed the refectory and adjacent rooms became part of a mansion.

Most of the abbey is only represented by low walls, pier bases and foundations but there stands high about half of a very fine lavabo (lavatory) of c1200 which is circular internally and octagonal externally with roll-mouldings on the corners and on the four surviving round arches of three orders. The wash-house was vaulted and had a large central pier attached to which were basins or fountains fed from a water tank over the vault. The building exemplifies the attitude of the Irish monks at Mellifont since buildings as fanciful as this were discouraged by the Cistercian General Chapter. The lavatory lay opposite the entrance to the refectory extending south from the cloister and formed part of a later southerly extension of the original mid 12th century cloister. A short section of cloister arcading nearby has been re-erected.

Projecting beyond the 12th century east range is a rib-vaulted chapter house of c1220 with set-back corner buttresses and several later medieval windows with floral tracery. The splendid doorway was taken off to a house in the 18th century. This room was entered through an older chapter house vaulted with a central pier. To the SE are traces of an infirmary. A lane separated the west range containing the lay brothers's rooms from the cloister west wall, this being a feature of several Cistercian abbeys in England, such as Buildwas in Shropshire. Some way to the NW of the church stands the northern half of a four storey 15th century gate tower.

The original 12th century church about 54m long internally with a nave 8m wide and a slightly narrower presbytery had a unique layout in that each transept had a pair of apsidal chapels which were set either side of a central square chapel. Equally unusual was the crypt under the west end, necessary because of the fall of the ground here and apparently not used liturgically. Rebuilding from c1230 to 1260 in which the presbytery and north transept were each lengthened by a bay did away with these apses, rows of three normal square chapels replacing them. Only the bases remain of the three east lancets. The north transept also gained a western aisle and its grand north doorway formed the main entrance as the fall of ground at the west end resulted in there being no doorway and porch there as was the norm. The nave had arcades of eight bays of arches carried on square piers and there were probably vaults over the aisles. The south transept was rebuilt c1320 after a fire and the crossing piers were later strengthened to support a central tower.

MONASTERORIS FRIARY   Co Offaly   610333   2.5km W of Edenderry

John de Bermingham founded a Franciscan friary here in 1325. Just one 14th century window now remains in a church 22m long by 7.5m wide internally with two blocked west windows probably of the 16th century. The blocked doorways below were for burial vaults built inside the church after it ceased to be used for parish worship in 1778. From here may have come the font outside Edenderry Catholic church.

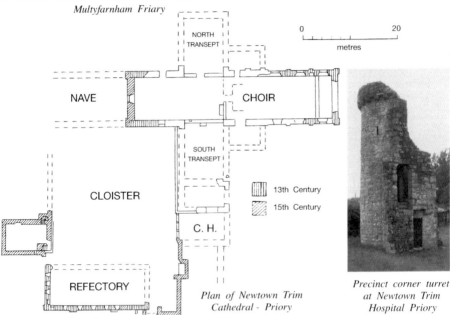

Multyfarnham Friary

Plan of Newtown Trim Cathedral - Priory

Precinct corner turret at Newtown Trim Hospital Priory

MULTYFARNHAM FRIARY Co Westmeath N402645 To N of Multyfarnham

This Franciscan friary was founded in the late 13th century under the partronage of William Delamer, the church being completed and dedicated to St Francis in 1306. A tall central tower and a south transept were added c1450. The friary was suppressed in 1540 but the friars kept returning to the friary even after periodic raids by the English authorities between 1590 and 1618. After being dispossessed by the Cromwellians in 1651 the friars moved to Knightswood nearby but they regained Multyfarnham in 1820 and gradually restored the ruined church. Currently medieval work only survives in the tower and the transept, the end wall of which contains the only remaining medieval window. The choir was entirely rebuilt as recently as 1975.

The church of the hospital priory at Newtown Trim

NEWTOWN TRIM CATHEDRAL PRIORY   Co Meath   N813568   1km E of Trim

The appointment of an Englishman, Simon de Rochfort, d1224, to the bishopric of Clonard resulted in the cathedral there being destroyed by the Irish. The bishop moved his see to a new cathedral priory of St Peter and St Paul built here within the protection offered by the nearby castle and walled town of Trim. The cathedral was served by Augustinian regular canons of the Congregation of St Victor of Paris and was a vaulted cruciform building 57m long with each transept having one east chapel. Parts of the east end still stand high with huge defaced lancet windows on each side and pilaster buttresses. In the 15th century the cathedral was reduced in size by crosswalls cutting off the transepts and most of the nave. Only the lower parts remain of a chapter house with a fine doorway in the east range of the cloister south of the nave. On the south side are the south and west walls of a refectory raised over cellars because of the fall of ground towards the river. Just one late medieval room remains of the west range.

NEWTOWN TRIM HOSPITAL FRIORY   Co Meath   N817568   1.5km E of Trim

In addition to building a new cathedral priory Bishop Simon de Rochfort also founded this hospital friary of St John the Baptist for Augustinian Crutched friars. It is set on the south bank of the river further east beyond the bridge. Three 13th century lancets remain at the east end of a church 36m long by 7m wide set on the south side of a small cloister. Most of the other features appear to be part of an early 15th century rebuilding. On the north side of the choir is a vaulted sacristy with a porch beyond it and one of several crosswalls in the church was evidently the base of a rood screen. A tower house with turrets at diagonally opposite corners stands beyond the west end of the church and may have formed the prior's residence. A range three storeys high ran north from it towards the river. At the NE corner of the cloister stands the northern half of a second tower, also with two upper rooms over a vaulted basement. The river was channelled to enter two out of a set of three vaulted rooms west of this tower. The buildings lay in a precinct with small round towers at the SW and NE corners. Some of the hospital buildings remained in use after the priory was suppressed and was granted to the Attorney General Robert Dillon. The site later passed to the Ashe family.

106   LEINSTER ABBEYS AND FRIARIES

Cathedral priory at Newtown Trim   *Newtown Trim Friary*

PORTLOMAN PRIORY   Co Westmeath   N132581   7km NW of Mullingar

A ruinous church with priest's chambers, now lacking any cut stone, is a relic of a monastery founded in the 6th century by St Loman on the west shore of Lough Owel.

ROOSKY PRECEPTORY   Co Louth   J190105   1km S of Carlingford

Parts of the north and west walls of a church once about 20m long and buried footings of a substantial domestic range orientated north-south to the west of it are thought to be the last remains of a preceptory of the Knights Templars.

SAINTS ISLAND   Co Longford   N071561   9.5km W of Ballymahon, very remote

Sir Henry Dillon founded this Augustinian priory before 1244. Of that period are the three round-headed south lancets and the piscina and aumbry below them, whilst the east window of three lights with intersecting tracery is 15th century. On the south side is part of an east wall with one window of an aisle or transept. Footings remain of the cloister on the north and fragments of a west range with vaulted rooms. One canon, Augustin Magraidin, d1407, compiled a collection of lives of Irish Saints which was still here with a few canons in the early 17th century when it was copied by the Four Masters, although officially the priory had been suppressed and granted to the Barnwells.

ST WULSTAN'S PRIORY   Co Kildare   N988338   1.5km NE of Celbridge

A tower, two gateways and other fragments within the demesne are relics of a Benedictine priory founded in 1202 and dedicated to St Wulstan, Bishop of Worcester, who had then just been canonised. After suppression it passed to John Alen from Norfolk.

SIERKIERNAN PRIORY   Co Offaly   N139022   8km SE of Birr

The church of an Augustinian priory founded c1200 is represented by its north wall and footings of the east and south walls, whilst the 14th century east window is reset in the Protestant church to the east. Crosses and graveslabs are relics of an older monastery. A vaulted flanker of c1580-1600 with gunloops has been added to the SE corner of the priory church and the surrounding earthworks may also be of that period.

LEINSTER ABBEYS AND FRIARIES 107

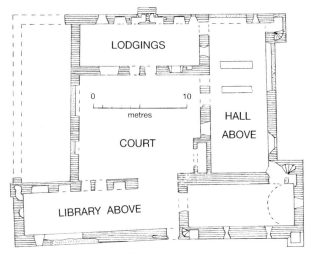

Plan of Slane College

Slane College

SLANE COLLEGE Co Meath N962752 On Hill of Slane, 12km W of Drogheda

An early 16th century parish church stands on the Hill of Slane and NE of it lies the ruin of a Franciscan college for four priests, four lay brothers and four choristers. Other colleges existed for priests serving major parish churches (a hall with a cross-wing still survives at Howth in Co Dublin), but nothing else in Ireland compares with the college at Slane, which is more like a castle with ranges surrounding a small court. The north range has obvious signs of lodgings with fireplaces and latrines. The east range probably containing an upper hall has a staircase turret at the NE corner but is otherwise rather ruinous. Very little remains of the west range. The south range contains the entrance doorway with a drawbar slot, over which was a probable reading or writing room lighted by pairs two-light windows with four-centred heads. The plaque over the entrance has the arms of England and France quartered. The SE corner is filled with a long three storey tower with a spiral staircase in a projection at the NE corner, probably the warden's house. Of a wall which at least partly surrounded the college there remains the gateway on the east.

In the grounds of the Flemings' seat of Slane castle is a 15th century hermitage with anchorites' cells in a block adjoining a small central tower of the dimunutive church.

Slane College

TIMAHOE PRIORY   Co Laois   S536902   7m SW of Stradbally

The exceptionally wide nave of a late medieval church was converted into a tower house and bawn after being granted to Richard Cosby in 1609. Just the east wall with the blocked chancel arch and the west wall with a central doorway now remain. It served a monastery or friary founded by the O'Mores. The nearby round tower is a relic of the original early monastery founded by St Mochua, d657.

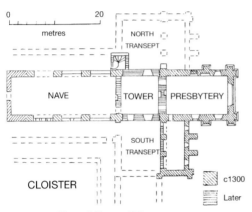

Plan of Tintern Abbey

TINTERN ABBEY   Co Wexford
S794101   5km N of Fethard

In 1200 William Marshal fulfilled a vow made during a rough sea-crossing by founding this abbey for Cistercian monks from Tintern in Monmouthshire. Of a new church of c1300 replacing the original one there survives the nave now shorn of its aisles, the crossing with a later embattled tower with corner turrets above, the choir with a huge east window once filled with Geometrical tracery, and the two vaulted chapels which lay east of the vanished south transept. These parts survived through having been made into a mansion by the Colclough family in the mid 16th century, many square-headed windows being inserted, and an embattled wing with a large south window being built over the chapels. The nave, fitted with cross-gables, and four levels in the tower remained occupied as a house until the mid 20th century. They have since been cleared and repaired by the Office of Public Works. Outbuildings to the SW incorporate a medieval gatehouse. Parts of a wall-walk and parapet remain on the choir. The nave has arcades of three plain pointed arches on square piers. A fourth and possibly even a fifth bay were probably originally designed but may never have been built, following a drop in the numbers of lay brothers after the Black Death. Excavations in 1982-3 revealed part of the footings of the east arcade of the cloister and a drain below the east range south end..

Tintern Abbey from the SW

Tintern Abbey

Former refectory range at Trim Abbey

110 LEINSTER ABBEYS AND FRIARIES

Armorial panel on the tower beside Trim Abbey refectory

TRIM ABBEY Co Meath   N803569   On NE side of town, N of river

Of the church of the 13th century Augustinian abbey established by Hugh de Lacy on the site of an older monastery there remains only the Yellow Steeple which lay on the north side of the choir and formed part of the reconstruction work after a fire in 1368 destroyed most of the abbey. It is a very tall structure almost 10m square with a SW spiral staircase within one of the clasping corner turrets. A squint gave a view of the high altar. The surviving belfry window is large and of two cusped lights with a transom. Further west is a smaller tower bearing the arms of Sir John Talbot, Lord Lieutenant in the early 15th century, evidence he was an important patron of the abbey. The three storey block east of it, still occupied as a private residence, appears to have contained the abbey refectory over a vaulted basement. On the south side near the east end is a vaulted oriel window which must originally have been the reader's pulpit.

The Courthouse stands on the site of a Franciscan friary of the early 14th century. There was also a Dominican friary founded in 1263 by Geoffrey de Genneville, then Lord of Meath. Most of it was removed in the middle of the 18th century.

TRISTERNAGH ABBEY   Co Westmeath N344610   12km NW of Mullingar

Two arches of a arcade are incorporated in a house of the 1780s and nearby is the heavily buttressed west front with a lancet over a doorway. These formed part of the church of an Augustinian abbey founded c1200 by Geoffrey de Costentin. Old descriptions suggest that a transept and a central tower with an octagonal top were added in the 14th century, which may also be the date of the arcade.

Wexford Augustinian Priory

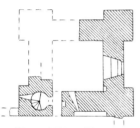

Plan of Trim Abbey tower

Wicklow Friary

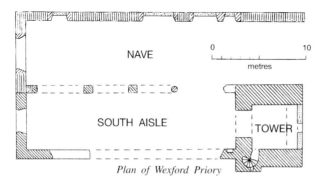

Plan of Wexford Priory

Tower of Trim Abbey

TULLY PRECEPTORY Co Kildare N734110 1.5km SSE of Kildare

The 13th century church with a central tower is thought to have served a preceptory of the Knights Hospitaller. The fragmentary nave and chancel each have one original window. The four arches under the narrower tower have all been blocked up.

WEXFORD FRIARY Co Wexford T047217 Near centre of Wexford

Most of this Franciscan friary founded in 1230 was demolished in the 1640s to provide stone for repairing the town walls. When suppressed the buildings included a tower, chapter house, dormitory, hall, kitchen and other buildings. The Franciscans recovered the site in the late 17th century. The existing church may incorporate older parts.

WEXFORD PRIORY Co Wexford T046221 Near Westgate, N end of Wexford

The Roche family founded this Augustinian priory dedicated to St Peter and St Paul before 1240. It is also known as St Selskar's, probably a corruption of the word sepulchre. It is a double naved structure with two complete arches remaining of an arcade of four with one round pier and two that are square. The windows are 15th century but the north nave must be 13th century since the heads of three lancets are visible above the large west window. The south nave with its arcade and tower with a SW stair turret may be 14th century. The tower remained in use to serve a church of 1811 beyond it.

WICKLOW FRIARY Co Wicklow T314940 To N of main street of Wicklow

Remains of a Franciscan friary founded in the mid 13th century are parts of the nave and the south transept with eastern altar recesses and a three-light south window.

OTHER MEDIEVAL MONASTIC SITES IN LEINSTER

ABBEYDERG Co Longford N141164 Site of an Augustinian priory founded c1205 by Gormgall O'Quin, Lord of Rathcline.
ABBEYDOWN Co Wexford S926618 Site of Augustinian priory.
ACAUN Co Carlow S900782 Footings of north-south domestic range with adjuncts on either side may be remains of possible Augustinian priory.
ARDEE Co Louth N965905 Moore Hall lies near site of the Augustinian Crutched friars' hospital of St John the Baptist possibly founded c1207 by Roger Pipard.
ARDEE Co Louth had a Carmelite friary but the precise location is not known.
    A chantry college building founded by Walter Verdun in 1487 stands at N959908.
ARKLOW Co Wicklow T245734 Park on site of Dominican friary founded in 1264 by Thomas Theobard FitzWalter. Parts of church and other buildings stood until 1750. There was also a short-lived Cistercian abbey at Arklow (at T248737).
ATHLONE Co Westmeath N040416 Modern Franciscan church on site of an old friary founded before 1241.
ATHY Co Kildare Site of St John's Priory of Augustinian crutched friars founded by Richard de Michael, Lord of Rheban before 1216.
ATHY Co Kildare Site of early 13th century Dominican friary.
BALLINABARNY Co Wicklow T141888 Site of possible post-medieval friary.
BALLYMORE Co Westmeath N222490 (approx) Site of Augustinian priory church of St Mary briefly used as a cathedral in the 1540s. Nothing now appears to remain of the nearby Cistercian nunnery founded in 1218 by the de Lacys.
BETHLEHEM Co Westmeath N086546 Last traces of nunnery close to L. Ree.
CLANE Co Kildare N879273 Effigy of founder Sir Gerald Fitz-Maurice Fitz-Gerald, 4th Baron Offaly , d1287, and other minor remains of Franciscan friary.
CLONAGH Co Laois S690830 Minor ruins of possible former priory.
CLONMEEN Co Laois S229740 Minor fragments and footings of possible priory.
CLONMORE Co Westmeath N360747 Slight traces of former nunnery.
CLONTARF Co Dublin O194364 Hotel on site of Knights Templar preceptory.
COOLCOR Co Offaly N529353 Site of Franciscan nunnery, a cell of Monasteroris.
COURSE Co Laois S417781 Excavation in 1901 exposed footings of ranges and church of a presumed priory. A rampart enclosed an area 80m by 70m around site.
DUBLIN O150339 Site of large Augustinian priory of St Thomas founded in 1177.
DUBLIN O151339 Site of hospital of St John the Baptist founded in the 1180s.
DURROW Co Offaly N321307 Site of mid 12th century Augustinian priory of St Mary. Older crosses and slabs nearby, and late medieval parish church rebuilt in 1802.
ENNISCORTHY Co Wexford S974397 Tower of Franciscan friary founded in 1460 by Donald Kavanagh remained standing until 1839.
FRANKFORD Co Offaly 179143 Catholic church containing late 16th century Pieta on site of Carmelite friary founded in early 15th century by Hugh O'Molloy.
GARRYCASTLE Co Offaly N027117 Supposed site of a medieval nunnery.
GRANEY Co Kildare S819840 Last traces of former nunnery.
HOLMPATRICK Co Dublin O256599 Ruined tower of later Protestant church on site of Augustinan priory transferred here from St Patrick's Island 2km to NE.
HORETOWN Co Wexford Location of Carmelite friary of St Mary founded by Furlong family in the 14th century. Exact site unknown.
KELLS Co Meath N7745758 Graveyard with 13th century female effigy marks site of preceptory of Knights Hospitaller probably founded by Walter de Lacy c1200.

KELLS Co Meath N737758 Site of Augustinian abbey of St Mary founded in 1180s
KILBRANEY Co Wexford S802187 Site of possible Tertiary Franciscan friary.
KILGLASS Co Longford N233650 C of I church supposedly on site of a nunnery.
KILLERRIG Co Carlow S814779 Farm on site of preceptory of Knights Hospitallers.
  Tower here was ruinous at time of 1540 suppression but in good repair in 1650.
KILMAINHAM Co Dublin O134338 Main Irish preceptory of Knights Hospitaller.
  Ruins survived until materials taken in the 1680s to build adjacent Royal Hospital.
KILMAINHAM Co Laois N478067   East gable and footings of church possibly of a
  friary. Vaulted chamber with trefoil-headed window on south side of nave.
KILSARAN Co Louth O508948 Knights Templar preceptory mentioned here in 1307
KNOCK Co Louth N924980   Mound 25m by 21m marks site of former monastery.
KNOCKTOPHER Co Kilkenny Possible remains of Carmelite friary in private house.
LEIGHLINBRIDGE Co Carlow S691654 Site of the first Irish Carmelite friary lay just
  south of castle. Suppressed in 1541 and the buildings later used as a barracks.
LISMULLIN Co Meath N933613   Earthworks mark site of Augustinian nunnery.
LONGFORD Co Longford   Site of Dominican friary founded c1400 by the O'Farrells.
MONATURE   Co Wexford T191684   Site of supposed Augustinian friary.
MOONE Co Kildare S790928 House of 1767 and 1846 on site of Cistercian abbey.
  It replaced an early monastery over jurisdiction of which was fought a battle in 908.
MULLENGAR Co Westmeath Nothing remains of the Augustinian priory of St Mary
  and the Dominican friary founded by William Petit in 1227 and 1237 respectively.
NAAS Co Kildare   Nothing survives of the Augustinian priory-hospital of St John the
  Baptist, nor anything of the Augustinian, Dominican and Franciscan friaries.
NAVAN Co Meath   Site of Augustinian priory of St Mary founded in 1189
  by Jocelyn Nangle. Ruins still stood in 1641. Effigy from here now at Slane Castle.
NEW ROSS   Co Wexford S718274 Theatre on site of Augustinian friary founded in
  c1270-1320. It had a hall and other buildings when suppressed in 1540.
NEW ROSS Co Wexford S717272 Site of Trinitarian friary founded by Wm Marshal in
  c1195. Later passed to Franciscans. Suppressed in 1539. Remains removed 1732.
OLDCOURT Co Laois S656873 Two walls with many narrow loops of possible friary
  church founded by the O'Moores on site of old palace of the bishops of Leighlin.
OLDLEIGHLIN Co Carlow S659664 Site of Augustinian priory of St Stephen, founded
  by Archbishop O'Toole in 1160s and ruinous by 1432 when it was suppressed.
ROSBERCON Co Wexford S716277 Site of Dominican friary founded in 1267 by
  Graces or Walshes. Had a dormitory and four chambers when suppressed in 1539.
  Old print shows church with tower, north transept and arcade of vanished aisle.
STRADBALLY Co Laois S573964 Franciscan friary founded in 1447 by O'Moores
  was demolished c1575 by Francis Cosby for materials to build a house.
ST JOHN'S Co Wexford S971382 Site of priory founded in 1230 by Gerald de
  Prendergast originally for canons of St Victor, later a cell of St Thomas at Dublin.
TAGHMON Co Wexford S919197 Footings of wide oblong church of early nunnery
  made Arroasian in 12th century but derelict by 1330s. Lay beside St Munna's Ch.
TERMONFECKIN Co Louth O141801 Site of Arroasian nunnery founded in 1140s
  by Donachad O'Carroll, and suppressed in 1539.
TULLOW Co Carlow S852731 Remains of Augustinian friary founded 1314 on older
  site demolished c1720. Had dormitory, hall, three chambers and kitchen in 1542.

CONNACHT ABBEYS AND FRIARIES

ABBEYTOWN PRIORY   Co Galway   M303506   3km SE of Shrule

Only the east wall and part of the north side remain of a long church of a small Premonstratensian priory said to have been a daughter house of Annaghdown founded c1260. Excavations in the 1980s revealed on the north side traces of the 13th century doorway and two much later structures thought to have been a transept with an adjoining sacristy. The only surviving windows are 17th century and secular in nature.

ANNAGHDOWN ABBEY   Co Galway   M287380   13km N of Galway

The church known as the "Nunnery" perhaps because it replaced a convent in use during the late 12th century is thought to have served a Premonstratensian abbey of St John which existed by 1224. Very little remains of the chancel added to an earlier nave. In the nave north wall there are two windows one above the other at the west end for a priest's residence, probably inserted in the 15th century.

ANNAGHDOWN ABBEY   Co Galway   M287379   13km N of Galway

This Augustinian abbey lies by the lake shore 150m SSW of the "Nunnery". Walls enclose a cloister 19m square with a refectory range on the south and an east range with a dormitory with opposed rectangular windows set over a series of five rooms, one in the middle being a chapter house. Another formed a sacristy adjoining the nave of the church on the north side. The west end of the church, including a doorway on the north side, is late medieval, but there is a small chancel with good late 12th century windows on either side. A third window facing east appears to have been reset in the parish church or cathedral higher up the hill. There is a latrine block at the SE corner.

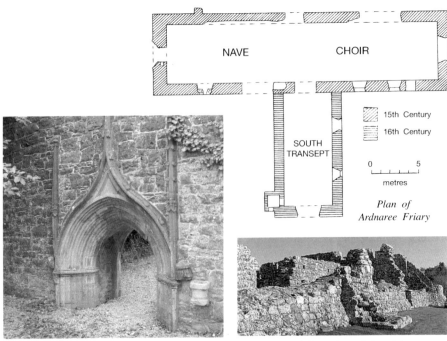

West doorway of Ardnaree Friary   *Annaghdown Augustinian Priory*

Plan of Ardnaree Friary

CONNACHT ABBEYS AND FRIARIES

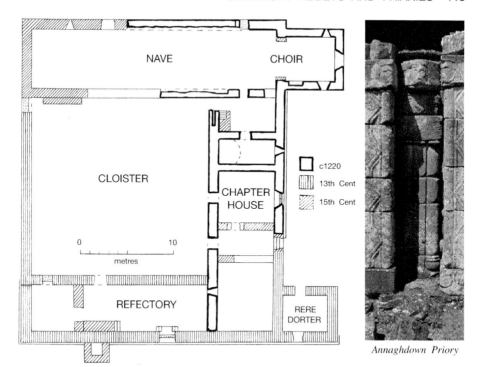

Annaghdown Priory

Plan of Annaghdown Augustinian Priory

ARDNAREE FRIARY Co Mayo G247188 On E side of R. Moy opposite Ballina
The O'Dowds are said to have founded this Augustinian friary c1375 but the only datable feature of the church is the fine west doorway which is more likely to be of c1475. A rise in the ground level makes it now seem low. It has a crocketed canopy and side pinnacles. The church has a later south transept. What looks like a latrine chute at the SW corner of it suggests a possible later conversion to domestic usage.

Annaghdown Premonstratensian Priory

Sedilia at Athenry Friary

Transept of Athenry Friary

West window

Plan of Athenry Friary

ATHENRY FRIARY   Co Galway   M504278   On SE side of Athenry

This Dominican friary of St Peter and St Paul was founded in 1241 by the 2nd Lord of Athenry, Meiler de Birmingham. Of that period are the nave with tomb recesses on the south side and the choir with a row of six north lancets. Although it lay within the walls of an Anglo Norman town and was the burial place of its lords the local Irish chiefs contributed towards the domestic buildings, none of which have survived their use as (or replacement by) a barracks in the 18th century. Felim O'Connor, d1265, provided the refectory, Eugene O'Heyne provided the dormitory, Cornelius O'Kelly the chapter house, Dermot O'Treasy the guest room and Art MacGallyly the infirmary. In the early 14th century William de Burgo and his wife Finola lengthened the choir and added a north transept, whilst another de Birmingham contributed the Lady Chapel, presumably the north transept. There was considerable rebuilding after a fire in 1423, when new arcades and a smaller east window were provided, along with a central tower which collapsed in the early 19th century. Chapters of the order were held in the friary in 1311, 1312, 1482, 1491 and 1524. It was suppressed and given to the town in 1574, having been exempted until them, only to be ransacked by the sons of the Earl of Clanricard the same year. The friars returned later and remained until 1652.

CONNACHT ABBEYS AND FRIARIES   117

Ballindoon Friary

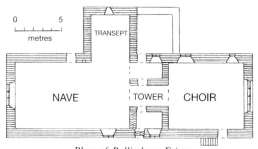

Plan of Ballindoon Friary

Ballinrobe Friary

BALLINDOON FRIARY   Co Sligo   G789149   7km SE of Riverstown

Set on a ledge beside Lough Arrow is a modest church which belonged to the Dominican friary of St Mary begun in 1507 by Thomas O'Farrell. It has east and west windows of four and three lights with intersecting tracery over sub-arches. A low gabled central tower is raised over a screen wall (see title page) which is itself gablod towards the north and south and contains two levels of openings. At ground level chapels flank a low and narrow passage, all three being vaulted at the same height. Above are the usual type of pointed tower arches with soffit ribs on brackets, one of which bears a rosette. There are lower round side arches also at this level and above these parts (which have tall side-windows) were attics in the roof spaces. Between this unusual structure and the north doorway a round arch has been inserted into an added transept. Access to the tower and screen upper rooms is by means of a stair cantilivered out from the choir south wall with a doorway at its foot for a former (or intended) sacristy.

BALLINROBE FRIARY   Co Mayo   M194648   On N side of Ballinrobe

The principal relic of this Augustinian friary founded in 1313 probably by the de Burgos is the east end of the church with a three-light window with intersecting tracery. Here in the friary in 1338 Eamon Albanach de Burgo (ancestor of the MacWilliam Iochtair Burkes) seized his cousin Eamon (son of the Earl of Ulster and ancestor of the Clanwilliam Burkes) and drowned him in Lough Mask 7km to the SW. The incident marked an important stage in the transformation of a branch of the Anglo-Norman de Burgo family into the Burkes, who adopted Gaelic speech and customs. .

118 CONNACHT ABBEYS AND FRIARIES

BALLINTOBER ABBEY Co Mayo   M154793   12km SSE of Castlebar

In 1976 a restoration of this cruciform Augustinian abbey church was completed in time for celebrations to mark the 750th anniversary of its founding in 1216 by Cathal Crovdearg O'Connor. During the restoration the 15th century west doorway, which had been removed to Hollymount in the 19th century, was restored in its original position. Much of the church is early 13th century but there was some rebuilding after a fire in 1264. The presbytery is rib-vaulted in three bays and has a triplet of short round-arched east lancets. The lancets in the nave are all modern but original ones survive in the pairs of chapels opening off the east wall of each transept. What remains of the cloister arcades on the north and east sides are 15th century but the enclosing walls and the east and south ranges are essentially 13th century with 15th century alterations and additions. The east range has next to the south transept a sacristy and also a library which opens off the cloister. Next comes the chapter-house with a good doorway and two wide east lancets. The rere-dorter or latrine at the SE corner of the range is a later addition. The abbey was suppressed in 1542 but the canons seem to have recovered possession after petitioning the Pope in 1635 for permission to do so. The church was unroofed and the domestic buildings damaged by Cromwellian troops in 1653. The Great Famine put a stop to an attempt to re-roof the church in 1846, but the eastern parts were eventually re-roofed in 1889. The nave remained a ruin until the 1970s and the former central tower has not been replaced in the rebuilding.

Ballintober Abbey

CONNACHT ABBEYS AND FRIARIES 119

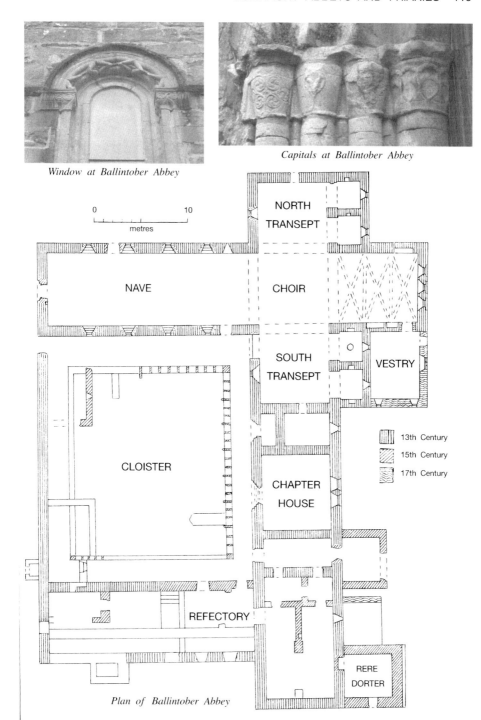

Window at Ballintober Abbey

Capitals at Ballintober Abbey

Plan of Ballintober Abbey

120 CONNACHT ABBEYS AND FRIARIES

Ballintober Abbey

BALLYHAUNIS FRIARY Co Mayo M498795 Between the station and the town.

The Augustinian priory incorporates parts of the church of an Augustinian friary of St Mary founded c1430 by the Jordan Macduff MacCostello family and burned in 1650.

BALLYMOTE FRIARY Co Sligo G661157 On north side of Ballymote

Papal licence was granted for the establishment of this Franciscan Third Order friary in 1444. It was burned c1483 and a hundred years later was "totally ruined", although it is said to have been taken over by First Order Franciscans in the 1640s and used by them for a about century. Over the damaged west doorway is a head with a three-tiered crown surmounted by a cross, probably a representation of a pope. Not much remains of the large east window and little except the openings to them of two projections on the south side shown in a drawing of 1779. One was probably a transept and the other a sacristy.

BALLYSADARE ABBEY Co Sligo G663297 0.5km NW of Ballysadare

Near the shore of the bay and hidden by shrubs and spoil-heaps of an adjacent quarry are the lower parts of a late medieval central tower and the older north wall of an Augustinian abbey church of St Mary which existed by the mid 13th century. In 1585 the church was described as partly thatched and there were two other ruined buildings and a dormitory, plus three cottages with gardens.

BANADA FRIARY Co Sligo 465101 G465100 4.5km SW of Tobercurry

All that remains of the Augustinian friary founded in 1423 by Donnchadh O'Hara are the eastern ends of the ivy-clad north and south walls of the choir. The latter has two sedilia with a twisted column between them and a hoodmould with ogees with moulded finials. There is also a doorway onto a passage and a straight staircase which led to a spiral staircase serving the central tower upper levels. Set on the north wall is a carved head with an elaborate head-dress. Lying nearby are parts of former windows and two gutterstones from the wall-walk have been re-used as gravemarkers.

CONNACHT ABBEYS AND FRIARIES 121

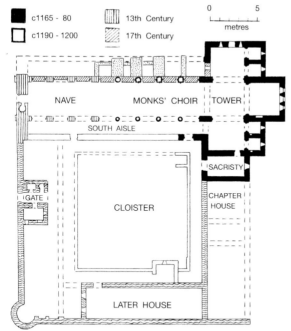

Plan of Boyle Abbey

Triple crowned head at Ballymote

Boyle Abbey

122 CONNACHT ABBEYS AND FRIARIES

BOYLE ABBEY   Co Roscommon   N806029   On N side of Boyle

Monks from Mellifont arrived in this area in 1148 but it was 1161 before they settled at Boyle and began work on the eastern parts of the church. It was unusual amongst Cistercian churches in having a central tower from the beginning, a structural device needed because of the very high arches into the transepts, off each of which are two vaulted chapels with round arched windows. The upper part of the tower is later. The presbytery is also vaulted and has three east lancets inserted in the 13th century in replacement of older windows. The eastern parts of the nave arcades probably of the 1190s differ from one another. On the south side are round arches of two orders on circular piers, whilst the leaning and now heavily buttressed north side has pointed arches on square piers with attached shafts. The octagonal fourth pier with remains of a bracket on the south and west sides of it marks the position of the pulpitum screen between the monks' choir and the lay brothers's choir to the west. West of here the arches are still round on the south and pointed on the north but are similar in style to each other with square piers with shafts. They probably date from between William de Burgo's attack on Boyle in 1202 and the consecration of the church in 1218.

Boyle Abbey

The abbey was the burial place of the MacDermots, who long remained important patrons and supplied it with several abbots. One abbot lost his office as a result of the "Mellifont Conspiracy" of the 1220s and the abbey's affiliation was changed from Mellifont to Clairvaux. Completion of the west front with its large ornate single lancet dates from about this period, when the abbey suffered another attack by Anglo-Norman forces under Richard de Burgo and Maurice FitzGerald. It may not have been suppressed until the 1580s when it was leased to William Usher. It was besieged by Hugh O'Neill in 1595 and given in 1603 to Sir John King. During this period the abbey became a semi-fortified house, losing most of the original buildings around the cloister except the sacristy next to the south transept, beyond which the lower parts of the chapter house doorway also survive. The outer walls of the west and south ranges were rebuilt to enclose a bawn serving a new house replacing the refectory on the south side, where ovens can be seen. A two storey gatehouse was built against the west wall with a porter's lodge flanking the passageway. The King family held the abbey until it became a monument in state guardianship in 1892, although in the 1650s it was briefly occupied by Cromwellian troops.

Burriscarra Friary

BURRISCARRA FRIARY   Co Mayo   M179765   12km N of Ballinrobe

Adam de Staunton of Castlecarra is thought to have founded this friary in 1298 for the Carmelites. The church is mostly 14th century with a west doorway and three south windows of that period, two SE corner buttresses, and a sacristy on the north side. The west wall of the east range may also date from that period. The friary was transferred to the Augustinians in 1413 and burned in 1430. Dating from after then are the south aisle with a two bay arcade with a square pier, the sedilia in the choir, the small east window inserted into the larger original one, and the rest of the east range, one room having a vault and another having a two-light window. Probably of 16th century date is the block with a staircase in its north wall in the SW corner of the cloister court and the footings of a crosswall with back-to-back fireplaces in the north range.

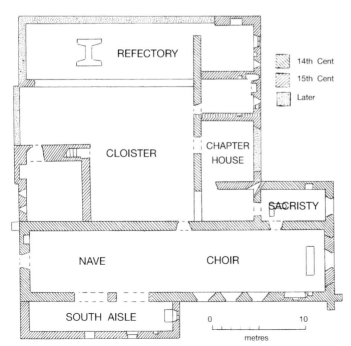

Plan of Burriscarra Friary

Transept end window at Burrishoole

124 CONNACHT ABBEYS AND FRIARIES

Burrishoole Friary

Burrishoole Friary

BURRISHOOLE FRIARY Co Mayo
L966955   2.5km NW of Newport
This Dominican friary was founded in 1486 by Richard Burke of Turlough, MacWilliam Iochtair, who later joined the community a short period before his death. The end windows of four and three lights respectively in the choir and south transept have intersecting tracery over slightly pointed sub-arches. There are also a pair of fine two-light windows with label hoodmoulds and sunk spandrels on the east side of the transept, where the altars would have been. The early 16th century central tower is as wide as the church for whole of its modest height. There are later gunloops in the transept west wall and others in the wall on the north side of the cloister. The west wall of an east range survives with a row of small loops.

CALTRA FRIARY Co Galway   M711430   At Caltra 6km SE of Mountbellew Bridge
A Catholic church of 1938 lies on the site of a Carmelite friary of St Mary founded c1320 by the de Bermingham lord of Athenry. It was suppressed some time before 1589 but c1737 was listed as having been subsequently restored. Rather confusingly there is also a tradition of there having been a nunnery here, probably before 1320.

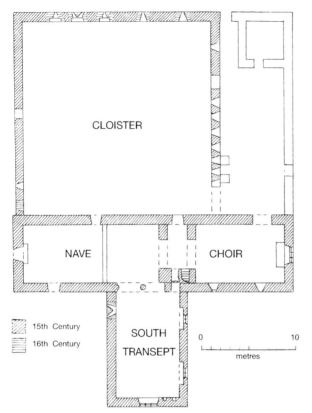

Window at Burrishoole Friary

Planj of Burrishoole Friary

Burrischoole Friary

CLAREGALWAY FRIARY Co Galway M371333   9km NE of Galway

On the north side of the River Clare are ruins of a friary probably founded by John de Cogan before 1252. The church has an inserted central tower, a nave with clerestory windows above tomb recesses and a choir with rows of lancets on either side with a piscina and sedilia below on the south and a canopied tomb niche on the south. A 15th century four-light window has replaced the original triple lancets of which traces remain in the east wall. The tower has stringcourses dividing the three upper stages, tall two-light windows in the top stage and double-stepped battlements with the corners raised up even higher to a third step.

The north transept with a pair of two-light east windows long remained in use for Catholic worship and was roofed until about a hundred years ago. Most of the west wall has gone and also the outer wall of the north aisle with a four bay arcade. The cloister to the south is rectangular rather than the usual square. The east and south ranges still remain. Both have been much altered with a lot of modern patching and some late 16th or 17th century fireplaces and neither retains datable medieval doorways or windows. Another building lies to the south and a mill beyond.

CLONKEENKERRILL FRIARY
Co Galway M131371
14km NE of Athenry

In the 1430s a parish church on the site of an early monastery was adapted for use by Franciscan friars. The east end of the church survives with a south window of two cusped ogival-headed lights under a hoodmould now blocked by a memorial. Two similar windows remain in the east wall of a south transept. Much of the choir east wall collapsed in 1983. An image of a bishop set on the stump of this wall is 18th century.

Claregalway Friary   *Stoup at Clontuskert*

CONNACHT ABBEYS AND FRIARIES 127

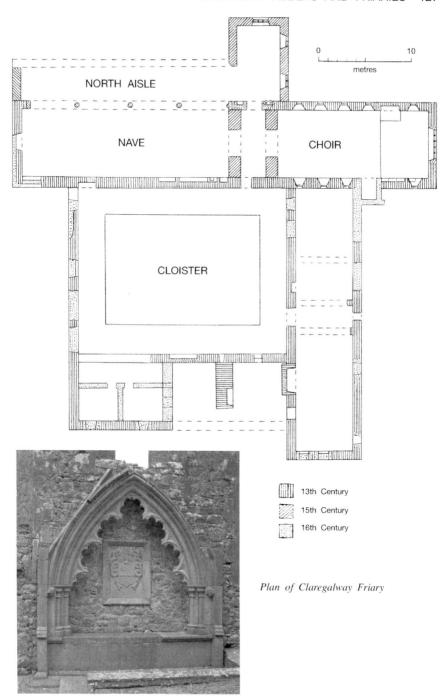

Plan of Claregalway Friary

Tomb recess at CLaregalway Friary

CLONTUSKERT PRIORY   Co Galway   M857258   5km S of Ballinasloe

In the 1140s the O'Kellys brought in Augustinian canons to take over an older monastery founded by St Baedan, who died c809. It became quite wealthy in the 13th century but the church of that date is just a plain oblong 34m long by 8m wide internally. One original lancet remains on the north side at the east end, and two on the south. The east range of the domestic buildings is also 13th century, with two original doorways and footings of a reredorter or latrine at the SE corner. By 1413, when it was burned, the place had just a prior and twelve canons. Rebuilding took much of the rest of the century. The best features are a five-light window with floral tracery and cinquefoil cusped lights which replaced the original three or five east lancets (traces of which remain), and a very fine west doorway of 1471 erected by Matthew MacCraith and Patrick O'Neachtain. The top panel enclosed by an inscription and pinnacles has figures of St Michael with scales for judging souls, St John, St Catherine and a bishop or abbot. Panels by the sides have motifs such as a dog biting its tail, two deer with intertwined heads and a pelican biting itself to provide blood to sustain its young, and there is a stoup on the north side. Just two years after this doorway was built the prior was accused of homicide and keeping concubines.

Also 15th century are the arcades of the small cloister, fairly complete except on the west side, the west and south ranges, the latter containing a refectory with its floor carried on a row of piers in the room below, and also the cross walls of the east range. A long transept with a three-light end window was built on the north side of the church, probably c1500. Only footings remain of rooms of uncertain purpose (chapels?) on the north side of the church and of a possible Lady Chapel projecting from the transept NE corner. The church was divided by a stone screen (see page 9) with two rows of four piers carrying rib-vaults. The wall east of this screen was inserted after the canons returned in 1637 and re-roofed the choir. The east range was also then still in use since its northern room has a fireplace of that period set in a deep projecting breast to contain an oven opening out of the back of it. Part of the nave south wall has been rebuilt since collapsing in 1968.

West doorway at Clontuskert Priory

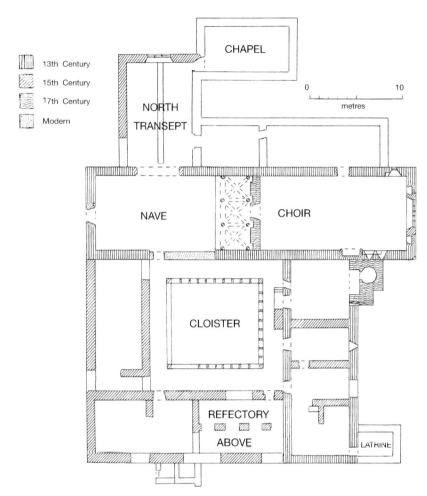

Plan of Clontuskert Priory

CLOONAMEEHAN FRIARY Co Sligo G613125 5.5km SW of Ballymote

Remains of a Dominican friary founded in 1488 comprise a short church with an east window of two ogival-headed lights fitted for internal shutters and a domestic wing north of the choir. The latter has traces of three rooms each with an east window. and a pointed vault with signs of wicker centering. Two corbels on the wing west wall are the only hint of a former cloister, and most of the north wall of the church is missing.

CLOONSHANVILLE FRIARY Co Roscommon M744909 13km SW of Boyle

The church of Holy Cross Dominican friary founded in 1385 by Mac Dermot Gall is very ruinous but it preserves a good east window and a small tower. It replaced or superseded an older monastery founded by Comitius, a disciple of St Patrick.

Chapter house facade at Cong Abbey

Detail of doorway at Cong Abbey

CONG ABBEY Co Mayo M146553
On SW side of Cong, N of Lough Corrig

Turlough O'Connor, King of Connacht was probably the founder of this Augustinian abbey of St Mary which seems to have replaced an earlier church burned in 1137. The cloister measuring 31m by 28m is the largest remaining in Connacht. Much of it has been rebuilt but the original parts are high quality work of c1200-20, which is also the date of the east range with a splendid facade for the central chapter house. A sumptuous central doorway is flanked by windows of two round-arched lights with a lozenge above under a round arch with a hoodmould. There is an even more elaborate doorway further south with chevrons and roll-mouldings. The small chamber north of it was perhaps a book store and the room beyond, next to the church, was presumably a sacristy. Only the east end of the church survives with triple lancets. Now set on the north side but originally on the other side facing the cloister is a very fine doorway of five orders with columns with good capitals. The arch was originally more obviously pointed. The large building to the SE of the east range was perhaps an infirmary. After being suppressed the abbey went to the King family and was later held in turn by the Binghams, the O'Donnells and the Brownes.

CONNACHT ABBEYS AND FRIARIES 131

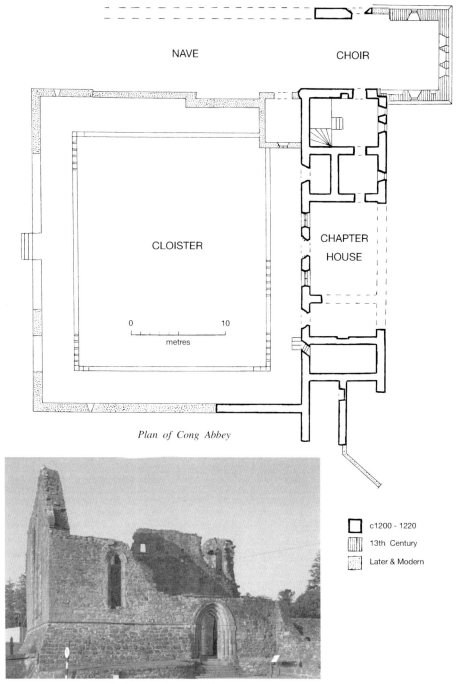

Plan of Cong Abbey

c1200 - 1220
13th Century
Later & Modern

North side of Cong Abbey

Creevelea Friary   *Creevelea Friary*

CREEVELEA FRIARY   Co Leitrim   G799315   0.5km W of Dromahair

Founded in 1508 by Owen O'Rourke and his wife Margaret, this was the last of the medieval Franciscan friaries to be established in Ireland and it is now one of the most complete. It was accidentally burned in 1536 and officially suppressed in 1541. There were still friars here in 1574 but in 1590 the Bingham family took it over for use as a stables. The friars returned in 1601 and repaired the church in 1642, only to be forced out by the Cromwellians. A later owner allowed the friars to recover the church with thatch in return for an exorbitant rent but they had probably left by the 1690s.

The buildings are set around a slightly irregularly shaped cloister 19m by 16m still with arcades on the north and parts of the east and south sides. Piers on the north side have carvings including St Francis with stigmata and an inscription across his body and another shows him in a pulpit with birds (with whom he was supposed to be able to communicate) perched in a nearby tree. The church is 36m long and 6.5m wide internally. It has a low central tower with a spiral staircase on the south side, and there is a long south transept with a large end window and two altar-recesses within the thick east wall. The choir has an east window of four lights and four south windows each of two lights. A doorway on the north side leads to a sacristy in the east range. The north range contains a refectory with single and two-light windows and remains of a reader's pulpit. There is a kitchen to the west and there are rooms with ovens in a later service wing which extends northward beyond the west range. This range has a small latrine projection. A larger latrine block serving the main dormitory lies at the NE corner.

CONNACHT ABBEYS AND FRIARIES 133

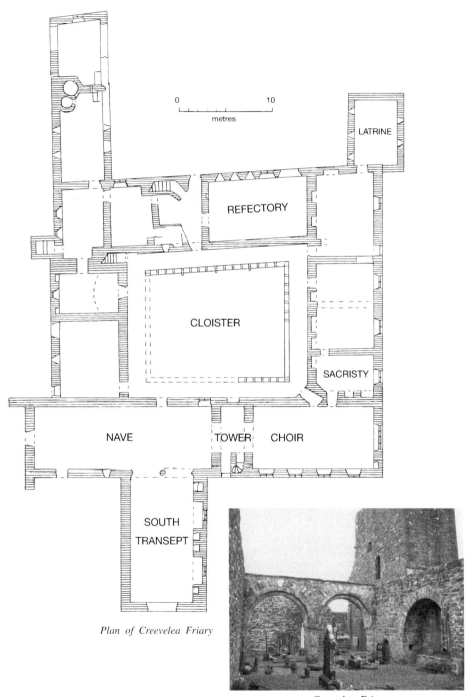

Plan of Creevelea Friary

Creevelea Friary

134 CONNACHT ABBEYS AND FRIARIES

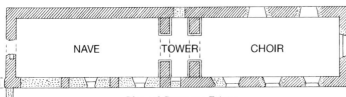

Plan of Dunmore Friary

DUNMORE FRIARY Co Galway M510634
Walter de Birmingham is thought to have founded this Augustinian friary in 1425. The church has a nave with a fine west doorway with a holy water stoup and a hoodmould with a crocketed head and pinnacles. There is a memorial tablet with the arms of the de Birminghams above it. Only an arcade of three blocked pointed arches remains of a former south aisle. The central tower is a later insertion. The choir was later converted for use as a Protestant church which remained in use until the early 20th century and its six windows all appear to be late 18th or early 19th century.

Dunmore Friary

EGLISH FRIARY Co Galway M813386 3.5km E of Ahascragh
This friary first mentioned in 1436 was a Carmelite house but it may have later been used by Franciscans. The 26m long and 6.5m wide church is rather overgrown and little now remains of its doorways or windows, although the four light east window survived until c1900. A pair of single light ogival headed windows remain in the east wall of the east range of the domestic buildings around a cloister to the north. The north wall of this range also remains. The feature at the NW corner may have been a latrine.

ERREW ABBEY Co Mayo G174123 7km SE of Crossmolina
In 1413 the Barrett family installed Augustinian canons here on a peninsular on the west side of Lough Conn to take over a late 13th century church with trefoil-headed windows and a piscina. It was given a new east window and a tiny cloister on the north with alleys only on the south and east sides. A dormitory with a NE corner latrine lay partly over the vaulted east alley. Other ranges enclosed the west and north sides, the latter irregularly set. Templenagalliaghdoo (church of the Black Nun), a nunnery oratory nearby to the north is a relic of a 6th century monastery founded by St Tighernan.

GALWAY FRIARIES Co Galway M296247 To SW, E and N of walled town
The present Dominican church of 1891 lies on or near the site of a friary, the choir of which was under construction in 1493. In 1570 it was "lately dissolved" but the friars later returned, if indeed they had ever left. It was converted in an artillery battery in 1642 and was destroyed in 1652 to prevent Cromwellian forces from occupying it.

In 1601 a fort replaced the Augustinian friary at M302250 which had been founded in 1508 by Margaret Athy and was described in 1578 as having been "late dissolved".

In 1296 William de Burgo founded a Franciscan friary at M297255, just north of the existing Franciscan church. By 1657 only the church survived, then in use as a court house. The friars re-occupied and repaired it in 1689 and 1723, and it was rebuilt in 1781. In the 17th century there was also a Franciscan nunnery at M294254.

There was a hospital of St Bridget founded c1541 by Thomas Lynch to the NE.

CONNACHT ABBEYS AND FRIARIES 135

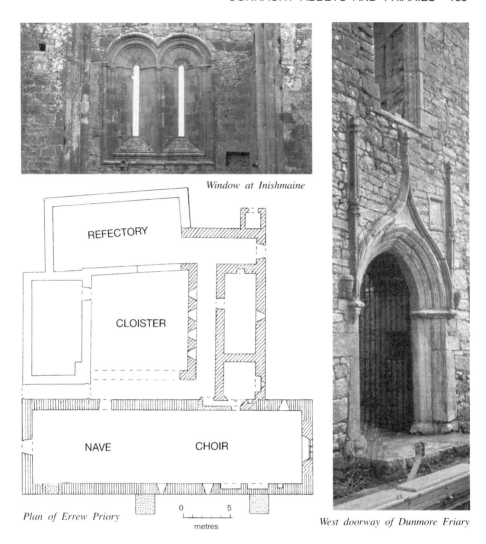

Window at Inishmaine

Plan of Errew Priory

West doorway of Dunmore Friary

INISHMAINE PRIORY Co Mayo   M139617   E of Lough Mask, 6km N of Cong
This Augustinian priory church has floral motifs on the capitals of the arch of four orders between the nave and the narrower chancel, which has two good round-arched east windows roll-moulded inside and out. Doorways on either side of the chancel lead into chapels with single east lancets. The nave has one south window and a lintelled doorway towards the east end of the north wall which looks like older work reset. The rest of the building looks c1200-10 but could just possibly be of immediately after the priory was burned in 1227 by Hugh O'Connor. This site, originally an island, had an early monastery founded by St Cormac. The building containing a passage nearby is said to have been the monastic gatehouse, but it looks like one end of a late 15th century tower house. It was probably intended to provide living accommodation.

KILCONNELL FRIARY Co Galway   M 733314   On N side of Kilconnell

This Franciscan friary on or near the site of an early monastery founded by St Conall is thought to have been founded in 1353 by William O'Kelly of Hy Many but the existing church does not appear earlier than the 15th century, which accords with the reconstruction said to be in progress in 1414. The friars became Observant in 1464. It was officially suppressed in 1541 but there were still six friars here in 1616, after a succession of tenants had held the lands, and they are said to have only been finally expelled just before the battle of Aughrim in 1691.

The church is 41.5m long by 6.3m wide internally and has a very tall inserted central tower with a spiral staircase in its north wall and upper windows of pairs of ogival-headed lights. The choir has a good four-light east window with intersecting tracery with a vesica in the topmost light. There are two-light windows facing south and a tomb recess of the O'Daly family in the north wall. Another tomb recess in the NW corner of the nave has figures of saints John, Louis, Mary, James and Denis. There is a south aisle with a two bay arcade. The late 15th century south transept also has a western aisle with a two bay arcade in addition to a pair of altar recesses projecting slightly from the east wall. An extra central chapel is a 16th century addition. Also 16th century is the sacristy with rooms for the guardian over it at the NE corner of the choir, but the meagre remains of the cloister and its ranges are 15th century. Part of the east range north end still stands high, and the east arcade of the cloister survives, but the fireplace on the west side is probably later. A 17th century mortuary chapel extends from the SE corner of the choir.

Kilconnell Friary

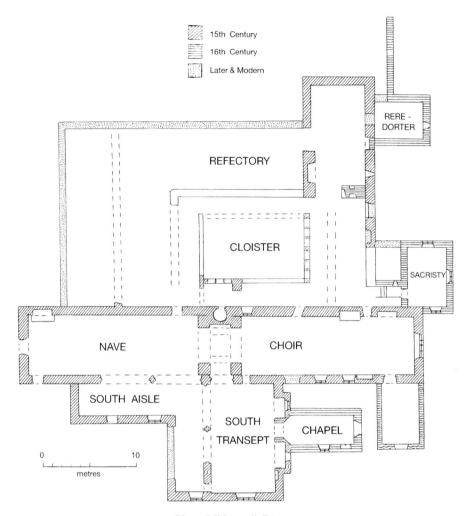

Plan of Kilconnell Friary

KILCREEVANTY ABBEY   Co Galway   M402574   6.5km NW of Tuam

Minor fragments remain of walls around a cloister 28m long north-south by 14m wide with traces of a possible south range and footings of a church composed of a nave with a narrower chancel. These buildings served a nunnery founded c1200 by Cathal Crovderg O'Connor which was originally Benedictine but by the 1220s had Arroasian Augustinian nuns. An inquisition of 1543 mentions the church as having a belfry and also lists a dormitory, hall, three chambers and a kitchen within a 2 acre precinct.

KILL FRIARY   Co Mayo   M262550   3km MW of Shrule

Minor ruins remain of the church of the earliest of the Irish Franciscan Third Order friaries, founded before 1426.

Kilmacduagh Priory

KILMACDUAGH PRIORY Co Galway M404000 5km SW of Gort

To the NW of the cathedral, two other early churches and the hall-house used by the bishop is another church which served an Augustinian priory. Named O'Heyne's church presumably after its original benefactor or first prior it has a chancel with a pair of good east windows of c1200-20 which are roll-moulded both inside and out. The nave is wider, although its width has been later reduced by building a new wall within the line of the original north wall, the lower part of which still exists. Extending south from the nave is a domestic range with three rooms including a sacristy and a chapter house below a dormitory. To the SW is another building, perhaps of later date.

KILNALAGHAN FRIARY Co Galway M739059 11.5km W of Portumna

John de Cogan established a Carthusian priory here c1250. It lasted only about 90 years and c1370 the site was taken over by Franciscan friars. The minor remains of the church enclose several memorials to members of the Burke family.

KNOCKMORE FRIARY Co Sligo G629070 3km NW of Gorteen

There are meagre remains, plus recent dry-stone walls, of a church 23m long by 6.5m wide of a Carmelite friary probably founded by the O'Gara family. The NE corner remains with the north jamb of the four-light east window shown on a drawing of the 1830s with tracery above sub-arches.

Knockmoy Abbey

KNOCKMOY ABBEY Co Galway   507436   15km N of Athenry

Cathal Crovderg O'Connor founded this abbey c1190 for Cistercian monks from Boyle. It was plundered by attackers in 1200 and 1228, and in 1240 the abbot was admonished for allowing a woman to wash her hair. The early 13th century 60m long church has an aisled nave, a presbytery with a ribbed vault and short transepts each with a pair pointed of arches opening into vaulted chapels. Two arches on each side remain of arcades of four pointed arches set between long lengths of solid wall, above which are single lancets forming a clerestory. In the 15th century the north, west and south arches of the crossing were walled up, and parts of the church perhaps then abandoned. The east wall has a single pointed lancet set above three round-arched windows of equal height. Another lancet above lighted an attic in the roof. Probably of c1400 are the wall paintings on the presbytery north wall, a great rarity in Ireland, and the sort of thing the Cistercians officially prohibited. Three Dead Kings and Three Live Kings are depicted over scenes of Christ with his hand raised in blessing and St Sebastion being martyred by archers. Little of the colouring remains within the black outlines. Some of the graffiti on the plaster of the presbytery walls are of great age.

Not much remains of the cloister but there are fragments of the refectory range on the south side and rather more of the east range with a sacristy next to the church and a chapter house which was subdivided in the 15th century when the number of monks had fallen. It originally had triple east lancets with chevrons on the inner embrasures. A later latrine block also remains. The building north of the church dates from after the abbey had been suppressed in the 1540s and Hugh O'Kelly had possession. The Blake family held the abbey from 1662 until the 19th century. See plan on page 140.

Knockmoy Abbey

140 CONNACHT ABBEYS AND FRIARIES

The nave of Knockmoy Abbey

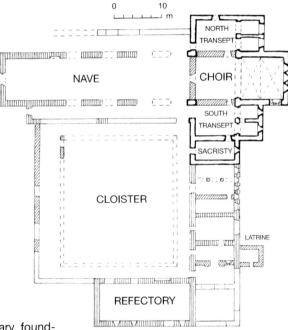

Plan of Knockmoy Abbey

LAVAGH FRIARY   Co Sligo
G563183   7.5km of Tobercurry

This Franciscan Third Order friary founded c1450 (known locally as Court Abbey) seems to have been an unusual joint community of both "brothers and sisters". The church is very ruined and overgrown with ivy, the west doorway being just a rough hole and the east wall missing. Later additions are the south transept with two altar recesses in the east wall and a window which had intersecting tracery facing south, and the ashlar-faced central tower. On the south side it has a belfry window of two ogivial-headed lights with sunk spandrels, a hoodmould and a transom. It once had a spiral staircase at the SE corner. A late 16th century survey mentions the church as having a thatched roof. There were also two thatched houses and a dormitory. There was a dependant church at Kilcummin 5km to the west, but this has now vanished.

Interior of Meelick Friary

LOUGHREA FRIARY   Co Galway   M620167   On N side of Loughrea

Richard de Burgo is thought to have founded this Carmelite friary in the 13th century, and the choir retains five pairs of lancets of that period in the south wall, but the five-light east window with reticulated tracery is 15th century, from which period most of the nave appears to date, and probably the south transept also. Certainly the lofty central tower is later medieval. It has a modern grotto in its base.

Loughrea Friary

MEELICK FRIARY Co Galway M943137 4.5km SE of Eyrecourt

The 15th century church of this Franciscan friary on a hill above the River Shannon is still in use as a Catholic church. It seems to have been founded by Breasil O'Madden and became Observant in 1479. It was officially suppressed in 1559 but continued to function under the protection of the O'Maddens. Original features are the west doorway, two arches for a former south aisle and another arch which once led to a south transept. The west window and the sacristy doorway appear to date from the early 17th century. Part of the east range survives beyond the sacristy, and there is also a later ruined house and a building with a stoup which may have been a chapel.

Cloister at Moyne Friary

MOYNE FRIARY Co Mayo G232289 3km ESE of Killala

This unusually complete friary for Observant Franciscan was founded in 1460 either by the Barretts or MacWilliam Burke. Work on it must have proceeded at a pace for a provincial chapter of the order was held here in 1464, first of a series of seven such chapters up to 1550. Sir Richard Bingham burned the friary in 1590 and in 1595 it was granted to Edward Barrett, but there were still six friars here in 1617 and one or two seem to have remained until c1800.

The church is 37m long by 6m wide internally and has a very tall and slender central tower. The west doorway is 18th century. On the south side of the nave is an arcade of four arches, three of which open into a later aisle considerably wider than the nave. The eastern arch opens into a transept with an arcade of two arches on the west and a thick east wall containing a tiny room between two deep altar niches, each with a two-light east window and a piscina in a corner of the recess. Other two-light windows lie in the south wall of the choir, where the east window is of four lights. Extending from the SE corner is a long narrow 16th century chapel. On the north side is a vaulted sacristy with its east end projecting beyond the rest of the east range. Beyond it is a vaulted chapter house with a pair of two-light windows. Next comes a passage running from the NE corner of the well preserved cloister out to where there is a ruined 18th century house. Beside this passage is a latrine block serving the dormitory above. Extending further north beyond here is a large refectory with the east wall having a pair of three-light windows set between one of two lights at the south end and a projecting bay containing the reader's pulpit at the north end. The oven in the SW corner is a later insertion. It backs onto the fireplace of a kitchen in the north range, beyond which is a wide set of steps up to the dormitories. The west range contains one long vaulted room (originally subdivided). The vaults to the north of it are probably of later date.

Inside the South Transept at Moyne Friary

CONNACHT ABBEYS AND FRIARIES

Moyne Friary

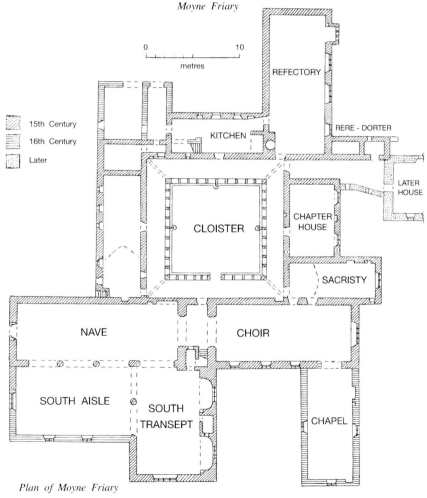

Plan of Moyne Friary

Arcades at Moyne Friary

MURRISK FRIARY   Co Mayo   L920820   11km E of Louisburgh

Hugh O'Malley founded this Augustinian friary by an inlet of Clew Bay in 1457. The church has some good windows and a doorway on the south side and an east window of five lights with trefoiled sub-arches below intersecting tracery. A vaulted tower was later inserted into the west end of the church, which is 27m long by 6m wide internally. After it collapsed the arch in the wall inserted to help carry the tower was blocked up. North of the church was a cloister. There is no evidence that west and north ranges ever existed but there is a fairly complete east range with a passage and staircase between the church and a narrow sacristy, north of which is a square chapter-house with an east window of two cusped ogival-headed lights under a label hoodmould. The dormitory above has a north end window of two lights with round sub-arches under below Y-tracery. The porch in the angle between the church and range is later.

East window at Murrisk

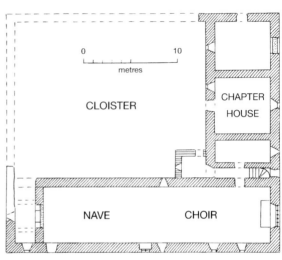

Plan of Murrisk Friary

Murrisk Friary

Murrisk Friary

PORTUMNA FRIARY Co Galway M854039 To the S end of Portumna

Until the early 15th century the Cistercians of Dunbrody maintained a chapel here. At the instigation of O'Madden, the local chief, they agreed to the abandoned building being taken over by Observant Dominicans as a friary, this being ratified by Pope Martin V in 1426. The original chapel with one lancet remaining on each side now forms the choir. It was given new windows of two lights on each side and a new four-light east window. The central tower is a slightly later insertion. The nave west of it is entirely 15th century and has arches on both sides into transepts. The northern transept forms the south end of a long domestic range extending far beyond the small cloister with re-erected arcading still remaining on the north and west sides. Probably the main dormitory lay in this range, with perhaps a kitchen below at the far end, whilst there are lower parts of a latrine turret facing west. The south range contains a refectory with two-light windows. The only remaining part of the east range is the sacristy at the south end.

Doorway at Portumna Friary

Cloister at Portumna Friary   *Window at Portumna Friary*

CONNACHT ABBEYS AND FRIARIES 147

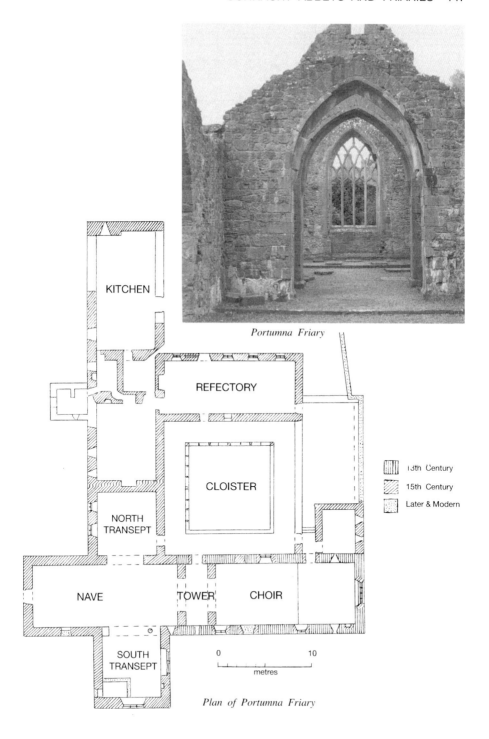

Portumna Friary

Plan of Portumna Friary

148 CONNACHT ABBEYS AND FRIARIES

Rathfran Friary

RATHFRAN FRIARY Co Mayo   G189329   3kim NNW of Killala

The church dates from soon after this Dominican friary was founded in 1274 either by the de Burghs or the MacJordans. The choir has trefoil-headed tomb recesses on the north side and five windows with pairs of lancets on the south side, whilst the east wall has remains of a large window and corner buttresses. Two single lancets in the nave were blocked up when a south aisle with a good east window was added in the 15th century. Just two doorways connect with the aisle as there is no arcade. At the NE corner of the church is a sacristy with an upper storey. North of the church low walls mark out the layout of a cloister 19m by 18m with an east range with four lower rooms (one retains a pointed vault), a north range with two rooms and a passage, and a single room west range with other rooms in western projections. The passage leads through to a northern outer court enclosed by service rooms on the other three sides. The friary was granted to Thomas Exeter in 1577 and was burned in 1590 by Sir Richard Bingham, Governor of Connacht, but friars remained in the vicinity until the 18th century.

Rathfran Friary

CONNACHT ABBEYS AND FRIARIES 149

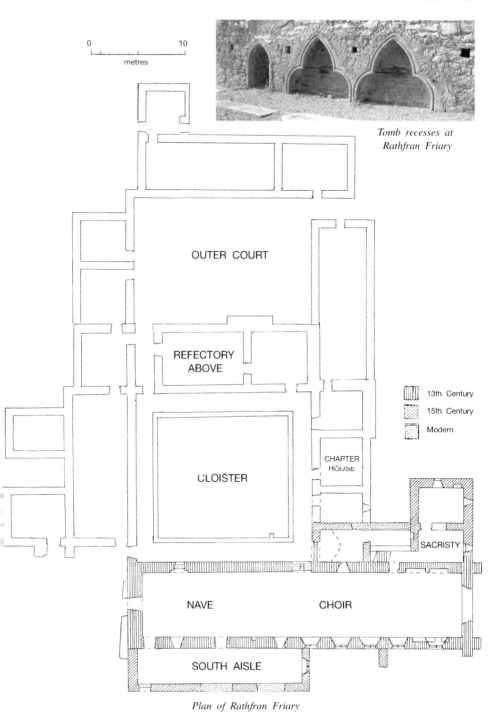

Tomb recesses at Rathfran Friary

Plan of Rathfran Friary

150 CONNACHT ABBEYS AND FRIARIES

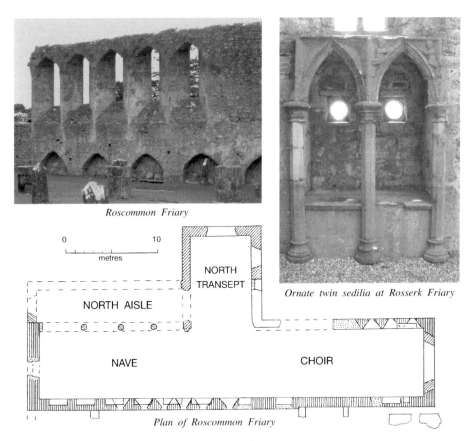

Roscommon Friary

Ornate twin sedilia at Rosserk Friary

Plan of Roscommon Friary

RINNDOWN FRIARY Co Roscommon M999549 14km NNW of Athlone

The small church of St John just NW of the wall of the former town belonged to a hospital run by Augustinian Crutched friars. One blocked lancet remains on the south side. The church has been shortened and given a west tower for later Protestant use.

ROSCOMMON FRIARY Co Roscommon M873639 To E of Roscommon station

Felim O'Connor founded this Dominican friary of the Assumption of the Virgin Mary in 1253. Of that period are the four lancets on the north side of the choir and the six lancets above a series of tomb recesses on the south side of the nave. An effigy of c1300 of the founder lies on a late 15th century chest (possibly of Tadhg O'Connor, d1464), on the north side with a series of niches filed with eight mail-clad warriors and angels above them. One of the warriors holds a battle-axe. There is another 15th century tomb recess on the south side next to a 13th century piscina. Other 15th century alterations are the windows (now damaged) which replaced lancets in the end walls, and the addition of the north transept, although the north aisle with its four bay arcade was probably added during the 14th century.

Roscommon also had until the mid 16th century an Augustinian priory which had superseded an older monastery founded by St Comman in the 6th century.

CONNACHT ABBEYS AND FRIARIES 151

ROSSERK FRIARY Co Mayo G254253 6km N of Ballina

Founded probably c1440 by the Joyce family, this is the best preserved of all the Franciscan Third Order friaries in Ireland, with a delightful coastal location. It was burned in 1590 by Sir Richard Bingham, Governor of Connacht. The church is 28m long by 6m wide internally and has a tall inserted central tower with the usual vault. The choir has a very fine east window of four lights with reticulated tracery with quatrefoils. There are two windows each of two lights on the south side, below the eastern of which are two sedilia with rib-vaulting over the recess and an octagonal pier on which is carved a light relief of a round tower. The nave has a good west doorway and a window above but no other windows. A single arch from it leads into a south transept with a three light end window and a thick east wall in which are two altar recesses, each with its own two light window. The recesses have angle piscinae and between them is a tiny storeroom. On the north side is a cloister without any signs of having alleyways. There are three ranges all of about the same size and each containing three vaulted rooms on the lower level, two of them in the east range being a sacristy and a probable chapter house. On the upper level the north range contains a refectory with a crosswall with back to back fireplaces dividing it from a kitchen, and the east and west ranges each have a dormitory with a latrine in an outer corner. If each window in their side-walls represents one cubicle then there were sleeping spaces for thirteen friars.

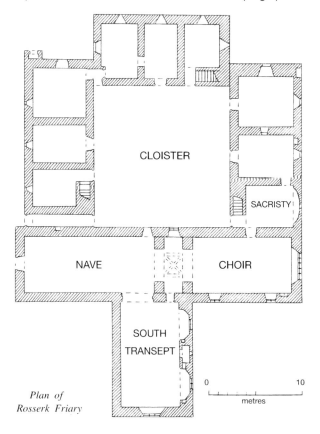

Plan of Rosserk Friary

Rib-vault of the sedilia recess

Domestic buildings at Rosserk

ROSS ERRILY FRIARY   Co Galway   M249483   2km NW of Headford

Although this Franciscan friary was founded c1351 by Sir Raymond de Burgo there is little evidence that any of the well-preserved buildings are earlier than the late 15th century when the friars adopted the strict Observance. The church has a good collection of the types of window tracery then in vogue. It is 38m long by 6.4m wide internally and has a high central tower with a spiral stair in its northern side which was inserted in 1498. The choir has four windows of two lights on the south, with a piscina below the eastern one. The altar was set in a recess below the five-light east window. A transept on the south side has a single arch to the nave, a doorway to a space under the tower and two altar recesses in the east wall. Between is an arch towards a projecting central chapel added in the 16th century. The nave south wall has three more arches, one towards a short aisle and the other two towards what is in effect a second transept with a two bay arcade between it and the other one. The Jennings family added a small chantry chapel south of the aisle in the 17th century.

The cloister has all four of its arcades preserved but is very small at just 12m square. As a result the east and west ranges continue further north alongside a second court. The parts of these ranges flanking the cloister have upper rooms set over the alleys, and there is the same layout on the north side. The lower room on the east side was probably a chapter house, with a sacristy between it and the church. The three storey block at the NE corner of the church also may have contained a sacristy, plus apartments for the guardian above. The refectory is located in the north end of the east range, with a latrine block beyond it, whilst the large kitchen with a big fireplace and a fish-tank lies at the NW corner of the northern court.

After official suppression the friary went to the earls of Clanricard who allowed the friars to remain. A chapter of the Franciscan order was held here in 1647. The friars were thrown out by the Cromwellians but later returned and stayed until the 1750s.

Ross Errilly Friary

CONNACHT ABBEYS AND FRIARIES 153

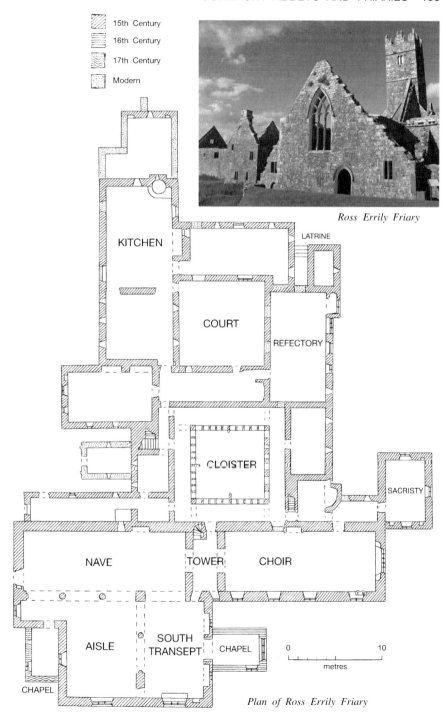

Ross Errily Friary

Plan of Ross Errily Friary

SLIGO FRIARY Co Sligo G694359 On E side of centre of Sligo

The choir of the church has a row of eight lancets on the south side and dates from shortly after Maurice FitzGerald, 2nd Lord Offaly founded this Dominican friary of the Holy Cross c1252. The friary managed to survive the conflicts of the late 13th and 14th centuries only to be destroyed by an accidental fire in 1414. Most of it dates from the rebuilding begun in 1416 with assistance from Pope John XXIII. In 1568 Queen Elizabeth agreed to a request by O'Conor Sligo not to suppress the friary on condition that the friars became secular clergy. The friary was badly damaged by Sir George Bingham's troops when they occupied it during a siege of the nearby castle. It was burned in 1641 by Sir Frederick Hamilton and later granted to Sir William Taaffe.

In the 15th century rebuilding a new east window replaced a set of lancets and a south aisle, central tower and rood screen were added. The transept may be as late as the 16th century. One of the older lancets is blocked by a monument of 1624 to Sir Donagh O'Connor, Lord of Sligo, d1609, his wife Eleanor Butler, and her daughter Elizabeth, d1623 by her first husband the earl of Desmond. A recess with tracery in its sharply pointed arch in the nave north wall contains a tomb of 1506 to Cormac O'Craian and Joanna Magennis. There a cusped ogival heads to the panels carved with St Mary and St John on either side of a Crucifixion scene. Other figures in the row include St Dominic in friar's robes, St Catherine with her wheel, St Peter with keys and St Michael with a raised sword and a shield. Other notables buried in the friary included Tiernan O'Rourke of Breany, d1418, and Brian MacDonagh of Tirerrill, d1484.

The cloister and its buildings are mostly 15th century but the sacristy and chapter house in the east range are 13th century. On the north side is an upper floor refectory with a reader's pulpit. An arcade pier in the NW corner has a carved head upon it. The dumb-bell shaped piers have various other motifs, one having a fluted spiral pattern.

Sligo Friary

Tomb at Strade Friary

Strade Friary

Sligo Friary

STRADE FRIARY Co Mayo   M259975   6.5km S of Foxford

In 1252 Jordan de Exeter at the behest of his wife Basilia de Bermingham transferred what had been founded as a Franciscan friary over to the Dominicans. The choir dates from that period, having a row of six lancets in the north wall. The other features of the building appear to be all 15th century. There are memorial slabs of interest in the sacristy and under the east window is a tomb desplaying a Pieta with two kneeling figures, but pride of place is taken by the really sumptuous tomb on the south side. Figures on the side include what are probably the Three Wise Men, Christ with his five wounds, St Peter and St Paul and a bishop with a cross. Above is a screen of complex tracery.

Tulsk Friary

TEMPLE MOYLE FRIARY Co Galway M539324 5.5km NE of Athenry

Minor fragments remain of a church of a Franciscan Third Order friary. There is said to have been a second church belonging to this order and founded by the Burkes c1441 at Tisaxon just 1km to the NW.

TRINITY ISLAND PRIORY Co Roscommon G833045 4km NE of Boyle

The so called Annals of Boyle were actually composed here in a Premonstratensian priory founded in 1215 by Maoilin O'Mulconry, a member of the main family of historiographers in Connacht. Ruins of a church remain on the island in Lough Key.

TULSK FRIARY Co Roscommon M833810 10km W of Strokestown

Only fragments now remains of the church of a Dominican friary founded in 1448 by the MacDowells. The chief feature is an arcade of two pointed arches into a transept.

URLAUR FRIARY Co Mayo M509894 14km N of Ballyhaunis

On the north shore of the lough are ruins of the church of a Dominican friary founded in 1430 by Edmund MacCostello and his wife Fionula, daughter of O'Connor Don, whose descendants were buried here. The community was reduced in the Cromwellian era when three of the friars were killed, two of them during the assault on Drogheda in 1649, and a fourth was in prison, yet in 1654 eleven Dominicans held a meeting here. There were still five friars in 1698, when they were forced to flee, and the last one is said to have lived until 1843. Old prints show the church as having a fine east window.

Altar recesses in the south transept at Rosserk Friary

OTHER MEDIEVAL MONASTIC SITES IN CONNACHT

BALLYNAHINCH Co Galway   Carmelite Friary founded by the O'Flahertys in 1356. Said to have been re-established in 18th century. Site now unknown.
CARRICKNAHORNA Co Sligo G763085 Slight remains of possible nunnery.
CLONFERT Co Galway M961211 The cathedral appears to have been served by Augustinian canons. An Augustinian nunnery also lay just to the south of it.
ELPHIN Co Roscommon Nothing remains of any of the medieval churches here, which included an Augustinian priory and a Franciscan friary as well as a former cathedral and a collegiate church.
JAMESTOWN Co Leitrim Franciscan friary of St Mary founded c1644 hosted synod of Catholic bishops in 1650. It was still in use in 18th century. Location uncertain.
KILLARAGHT Co Sligo M769983 Site of parochial church and a nunnery and hospital of which some buildings still stood in the 1680s.
KILLEANY Co Galway L886071 Site of Franciscan friary founded on 1485. Robbed of materials to build Arkin Castle down on the shore below.
MOHILL Co Leitrim H090969 Later church on site of monastery which later became Augustinian. Was parochial by 1470. Chapel added c1610. No remains of interest.
TEMPLEHOUSE Co Sligo Named after a preceptory of the Knights' Templar. 13th century hall-block of castle might possibly have belonged to them.
TOOMBEOLA Co Galway M761439 Small later church on site of Dominican friary founded in 1427. Supposedly destroyed to build Ballynahinch castle.
TUAM Co Galway M432519 Roadside plaque in housing estate marks site of Premonstratensian priory founded c1203 by William de Burgo. Mostly removed in 1791.
TUAM Co Galway M436518 Site of Augustinian hospital-priory founded c1140 by Turlough O'Connor and upgraded as an abbey c1360. In use until at least 1574.

GLOSSARY OF TERMS

Aisle	-	A passage beside part of a church.
Antae	-	Projections of north and south walls of a church beyond the end gables.
Apse	-	A semicircular chapel or similarly shaped east end of a church.
Ashlar	-	Masonry of large blocks cut to even faces and square edges.
Architrave	-	A moulding above or on either side or a doorway.
Chancel	-	The eastern chamber of a church reserved for priests and choristers.
Chevrons	-	Vs usually arranged in a continuous sequence to form a zig-zag.
Choir	-	The part of a monastic church containing the monks' stalls
Clerestory	-	An upper storey pierced by windows lighting the floor below.
Corbel	-	A projecting or overhanging stone.
Crockets	-	Leafy knobs on the edge of the top of a window, doorway or recess.
Cruciform Church	-	Cross shaped church with transepts forming the arms of the cross.
Cusps	-	Projecting points between the foils of a foiled Gothic arch.
Dog Tooth	-	Four-cornered stars placed diagonally and raised pyramidally.
Easter Sepulchre	-	A recess in a chancel which received an effigy of Christ at Easter.
Foil	-	A lobe formed by the cusping of a circle or arch.
Head Stops	-	Heads of humans or beasts forming the ends of a hoodmould.
Hood-Moulding	-	A narrow band of stone projecting out over a window or doorway.
Impost	-	A wall bracket, often moulded, to support one end of an arch.
Jamb	-	The side of a doorway, window or other opening.
Lancet	-	A long and comparatively narrow window. Usually pointed headed.
Lavabo	-	A lavatory or washing place, usually next to the refectory entrance.
Lintel	-	A horizontal stone or beam spanning an opening.
Machicolation	-	Slot in the floor of a turret, etc, allowing missiles to be dropped down.
Mullion	-	A vertical member dividing the lights of a window.
Nave	-	The part of a church in which the congregation stood or sat.
Ogee-headed window	-	Topped by a curve which is partly convex and partly concave.
Oratory	-	A chapel just large enough to contain a priest and two or three others.
Piscina	-	A stone basin used for rinsing out holy vessels after mass.
Presbytery	-	The part of a monastic church containing the high altar.
Prior	-	The head of a priory or the deputy head of an abbey.
Rere-arch	-	An arch on the inside face of a window embrasure or doorway.
Rere-dorter	-	A latrine situated at the far end of a monastic dormitory
Respond	-	A half-pier or column bonded into a wall and carrying an arch.
Reticulation	-	Tracery with a net-like appearance.
Romanesque	-	Architectural style using round arches. Current in 11th-12th centuries.
Rood Screen	-	A screen with a crucifix mounted upon it between a nave and chancel.
Round Tower	-	Slender 10th, 11th or 12th century tower used as a refuge & bell-tower.
Sacristy	-	A part of a church where vestments and sacred vessels were kept.
Sedilia	-	Seats for clergy (usually three) in the south wall of a chancel.
Spandrel	-	The surface beteen two arches or between an arch and a corner.
Transept	-	A cross-arm projecting at right angles from the main body of a church.
Trefoiled	-	Composed of three segments of circles.
Tympanum	-	The space between the lintel of a doorway and the arch above it.
Wall - Walk	-	A walkway on top of a wall, always protected by an outer parapet.
Vesica Window	-	A pointed oval or eye-shaped opening.
Warming House	-	The only room in an abbey (other than a kitchen) with a fireplace.

FURTHER READING

An Anglo - Norman Monastery (Bridgetown), Tadhg O'Keefe, 1999
Archaeological inventories based on the National Monument Records - vols for
 Carlow, Cavan, Cork, Galway West & North, Laois, Leitrim, Louth, Meath
 Monaghan, Offaly, Sligo South, Tipperary North, Waterford, Wexford, Wicklow
Architecture and Sculpture in Ireland, Roger Stalley, 1971
Buildings of Ireland series: vols for NW Ulster, NW Leinster, Dublin, 1979, 1993, 2005
Cathedrals of Ireland, Peter Galloway, 1992
Cistercian Monasteries, Roger Stalley, 1989
Guide to the National Monuments of Ireland, Peter Harbison, 1970
Irish Churches and Monastic Buildings, 3 vols, Harold Leask, 1955, 1958, 1960
Medieval Churches of Ireland, Mike Salter, 2009 See note below.
Religious Houses: Ireland, A. Gwynne & N.D. Hadcock, 1970
The Architecture of Ireland from the earliest times to 1880, Maurice Craig, 1982
The Castles of Leinster, Mike Salter, 2004 (Details of towers of outer court at Kells)
The Churches and Abbeys of Ireland, Brian de Breffney & George Mott, 1976
The Shell Guide to Ireland, Lord Killanin and Michael V. Duignan, 1962
See also articles in the annual journals of Cork Historical & Archaeological Society,
 Irish Historical Studies, Royal Society of Antiquaries of Ireland, Ulster Journal of
 Archaeology, etc

See companion volume Medieval Churches of Ireland for plans of the Augustinian churches at Duleek and Dungiven, also of cathedral-priories at Downpatrick and Dublin, and for details of other churches used by Augustinian regular canons at Drumlane and Monaincha.

Church at Toomevara, Co Cork

Franciscan Friary (French Church) at Waterford   *Church at Bridgetown, Co Cork*

INDEX OF IRISH MEDIEVAL MONASTERIES

FRIARS: AF - Augustinian, CF - Carmelite, DF - Dominican FF - Franciscan (*Third Order)
MILITARY ORDERS: KH - Knights Hospitaller, KT - Knights Templar
MONKS: BM - Benedictine, CM - Cistercian, TM - Tironesian
NUNS: AN - Augustinian, CN - Cistercian, FN - Franciscan
REGULAR CANONS AC - Augustinian, PC - Premonstratensian, TC - Trinitarian

Abbeyderg AC 78	Caltra CF 124	Errew AC 134-135	Kilsaran KT 113	Old Leighlin AC 113
Abbeydorney CM 32	Canon Island AC 47	Fermoy CM 53	Kilshanny AC 63	Omagh FF 31
Abbeydown AC 112	Carlingford DF 82	Ferns AC 90	Kilteel KH 100	Portloman AC 106
Abbeyfeale CM 77	Carrickfergus FF 31	Fethard AF 53	Kinsale CF 63	Portumna DF 146-14
Abbeyshrule CM 78	Carrickmagriffin FF 47	Fore BM 90-91	Knockmore CF 138	Quin FF 70-71
Abbeytown PC 114	Cashel DF 48	Frankford CF 112	Knockmoy CM 138-140	Rathfran DF148-149
Acaun AC 112	Cashel FF 48	Gallen AC 92	Knockavery AN 77	Rathkeale AC 72
Adare TC 32	Castlecor 77	Galway AF 134	LLambeg FF 31	Rathmullan CF 30-3
Adare AF 32-33	Castledermot AF 82	Galway DF 134	Laragh CM 100	Rattoo AC 72-73
Adare FF 34-35	Castledermot FF 82	Galway FF 134	Lavagh FF* 140	Rincrew KT 72
Aghmanister 77	Castlelyons CF 48-49	Gill (Cork) AC 51	Legan BM 77	Rinndown AF 150
Aghaboe AP 78-79	Cavan FF 31	Glanworth DF 53	Leighlinbridge CF 113	Roscommon DF 150
Aghaboe DF 78-79	Chore AC 77	Glanawydan CM 77	Limerick DF 63	Roscrea FF 72-73
Annaghdown AC 114-115	Clareabbey AC 49	Glascarrig TM 92	Lisgoole AC 28	Rosbercon DF 113
Annaghdown PC 114-115	Claregalway FF 126-127	Glenarm FF* 23	Lislaughtin FF 63	Roosky KT 106
Ardee AF 112	Coleraine DF 31	Glendalough AC 92	ismullin AN	Ross BM 73
Ardee CF 112	Clonfert AC 157	Grace Dieu AN 93	Longford DF	Rosserk FF* 150-151
Ardfert FF 36-37	Clonkeenkerrill FF 126	Great Connell AC 93	Lorrha AP 64-65	Ross Errily FF 152-1
Ardfinnan CF 36	Clonmacnoise AN 83	Grey CM 24-25	Lorrha DF 64-65	Saints' Island AC 10
Ardnaree AF 114-115	Clonmel FF 49	Holy Cross 54-55	Lough Derg AF 31	St Wulstan's BM 106
Arklow DF 112	Clonmines AF 83	Hollywood FF 31	Loughrea CF 140-141	Sherkin FF 73
Armagh AC 31	Clonosey FF 31	Holmpatrick AC 112	Louth AC 101	Sierkernan AC 106
Armagh DF 20-21	Clontuskert AC 128-129	Hore CM 56-57	Magherabeg FF* 28-29	Slane FF 107
Askeaton AC 36, 39	Cloonamehan DF 129	Horetown CF 112	Magheraglass AP 29	Sligo DF 154-155
Askeaton FF 38-39	Cloonshanville DF 129	Inch CM 26-27	Mahon CM 65	St John's AC 113
Assaroe CM 20	Comber CM 31	Inchicronan AC 56	Meelick FF 140	Stradbally FF 113
Athassel AC 40-41	Cong AC 130-131	Inchmore AC 93	Mellifont CM 102-103	Strade DF 155
Athenry DF 116	Coolcor FN 112	Inishmaine AC 135	Mohill AC 157	Taghmon AN 113
Athlone FF 112	Corbally AC 49	Inislounaght CM 58	Molana AC 65	Templehouse KT 157
Athy AF 112	Corcomroe CM 50-51	Inistioge AC 93	Molough AN 77	Temple Moyle FF* 15
Athy DF 112	Cork AF 51	Innisfallen AC 58	Monaghan FF 31	Termonfeckin AN 11:
Balleegham FF 20	Cork DF 51	Jerpoint CM 94-95	Monasteranenagh CM 66	Thurles CF 73
Ballindoon DF 117	Cork FF 51	Kells (Ulster) AC 31	Monasternagalliaghduff	Timahoe 108
Ballinrobe AF 117	Corrickmore FF* 21	Kells AC 96-97	AN 66-67	Timoleagh FF 74-75
Ballinskelligs AC 42-43	Course AC 112	Kells AC 112	Monasteroris FF 103	Tintern CM 108-109
Ballintober AC 118-119	Creevelea FF 132-133	Kells KH 112	Monature AC 113	Tivea Lough FF 31
Ballybeg AC 42	erry AF 31	Kilbarry KT 77	Moone CM 113	Toombeola DF 157
Ballyboggan AC 79	Devenish AC 22	Kilbraney FF* 112	Moor FF 67	Toomevara AC 76
Ballyhaunis AC 120	Donegal FF 22-23	Kilconnell FF 136-137	Mothel AC 67	Tracton CM 77
Ballymacadane AN 43	Downpatrick CN 31	Kilcooly CM 59	Mourne KH 67	Trim AC 109-110
Ballymore AC 112	Drogheda AC 84-85	Kilcrea FF 60-61	Movilla AC 29	Trinity PC
Ballymote FF* 120	Drogheda DF 84-85	Kilcreevanty AN 137	Moyne FF 141-143	Trinity Island PC 156
Ballynahinch CF 157	Dublin AC 84-85	Kilcullen FF 97	Muckamore AC 31	Tristernagh AC 110
Ballysadare AC 120	Dublin AC 112	Kildare FF 98	Muckross 68-69	Tuam AC 157
Ballysaggart FF* 20	Dublin 112	Kilkenny AC 98-99	Mullengar AC 113	Tuam PC 157
Baltinglass CM 78-79	Dublin CM 84	Kilkenny DF 99-100	Multifarnham FF 104	Tullow AF 113
Banada AF 120	Duiske CM 86-87	Kilkenny FF 99	Murrisk AF 144-145	Tully KH 111
Bangor AC 21	Duleek AC	Kill FF* 137	Naas AC 113	Tulsk DF 156
Bantry 77	Dunbrody CM 88-89	Killagha AC 61	Naas AF 113	Tyone AF 76
Bective CM 80-81	Dundalk AF 89	Killeany FF 157	Naas DF 113	Urlaur DF 156
Bethlehem 112	Dundalk FF 88-89	Killeigh AC 100	Naas FF 113	Waterford AC 76
Bonamargy FF* 20-21	Dungarvan AC 52-53	Killerrig KH 113	Navan AC 113	Waterford AC 76,159
Boyle CM 121-122	Dungiven AC 23	Killone AN 61	Nenagh FF 68-69	Waterford DF 76
Bridgetown AC 44	Dunmore 134-135	Killydonnell FF* 26, 28	New Ross AF 113	Wexford AC 110-111
Burriscarra CF 123	Elphin AC 157	Kilmacrenan FF* 26	New Ross TF 113	Wexford FF 111
Burrishoole DF 124-125	Elphin FF 157	Kilmacduagh AC 128	Newry CM 31	Wicklow FF 111
Buttevant FF 44-45	Ennis FF 52	Kilmallock DF 62	Newtown Trim AC 104	Youghal DF 77
Cahir AC 46-47	Eglish CF 134	Kilmainham KH 113	Newtown Trim AF 104	Youghal FF 77
Callan AF 80	Erenagh CM 31	Kilnalaghan FF 138	Newtownards DF 28-29	